Implementing Azure C
Design Patterns

Implement efficient design patterns for data management,
high availability, monitoring, and other popular patterns on
your Azure Cloud

Oliver Michalski
Stefano Demiliani

BIRMINGHAM - MUMBAI

Implementing Azure Cloud Design Patterns

Commissioning Editor: Gebin George
Acquisition Editor: Heramb Bhavsar
Content Development Editor: Nithin Varghese
Technical Editor: Komal Karne
Copy Editor: Safis Editing
Project Coordinator: Virginia Dias
Proofreader: Safis Editing
Indexer: Francy Puthiry
Graphics: Tom Scaria
Production Coordinator: Melwyn Dsa

First published: January 2018

Production reference: 1250118

Published by Packt Publishing Ltd.
Livery Place
35 Livery Street
Birmingham
B3 2PB, UK.

ISBN 978-1-78839-336-2

www.packtpub.com

I would like to dedicate this book to my little daughter, Sara: I love you! maybe one day you will be proud of me for this!

– Stefano Demiliani

`mapt.io`

Mapt is an online digital library that gives you full access to over 5,000 books and videos, as well as industry leading tools to help you plan your personal development and advance your career. For more information, please visit our website.

Why subscribe?

- Spend less time learning and more time coding with practical eBooks and Videos from over 4,000 industry professionals

- Improve your learning with Skill Plans built especially for you

- Get a free eBook or video every month

- Mapt is fully searchable

- Copy and paste, print, and bookmark content

PacktPub.com

Did you know that Packt offers eBook versions of every book published, with PDF and ePub files available? You can upgrade to the eBook version at `www.PacktPub.com` and as a print book customer, you are entitled to a discount on the eBook copy. Get in touch with us at `service@packtpub.com` for more details.

At `www.PacktPub.com`, you can also read a collection of free technical articles, sign up for a range of free newsletters, and receive exclusive discounts and offers on Packt books and eBooks.

Contributors

About the authors

Oliver Michalski started his IT career in 1999 as a web developer. Now, he is a senior software engineer for Microsoft .NET and an SOA architect. He also works as an independent enterprise consultant in the field of Microsoft Azure. When he started with Microsoft Azure in 2011, there was no Azure community in Germany. Therefore, Oliver founded Azure Community Germany (ACD).

Oliver has been the chairman of the ACD, since April 2016, and since July 2017 he has been a Microsoft Most Valuable Professional for Microsoft Azure.

Stefano Demiliani is a Microsoft Certified Solution Developer (MCSD) and a long-time expert on different Microsoft technologies. He has a master's degree in computer engineering from Politecnico of Turin. He works as a CTO for EID/Navlab (Microsoft partner in Italy) and he's frequently involved on helping customers on moving their business to the Azure cloud.

He has worked with Packt for many IT books and he's the author of *Building ERP solutions with Microsoft Dynamics NAV*, a hands-on guide to building enterprise architectures based on the Microsoft Dynamics NAV ERP and the Azure platform.

> *This book is a dream that has come true (the cloud is my passion and writing a book about Azure is for me a reached target). Thanks to all the wonderful staff that has worked with me over these months, and thanks also to my family (I'll return to you all the hours spent working on this book).*

About the reviewer

Florian Klaffenbach started his IT career in 2004 as first- and second-level IT support technician and IT salesman trainee for a B2B online shop. Since then, he has taken several steps from IT admin, to support agent, to community manager, and cloud architect at Dell and CGI, and then ended up as a technology solutions professional for Microsoft in 2017. In April 2016, he was awarded the Microsoft Most Valuable Professional, honoring his work for the IT community.

I want to thank the team at Packt for giving me the chance to review the book, as well as my little family for letting me invest the time I had into these projects.

Packt is searching for authors like you

If you're interested in becoming an author for Packt, please visit `authors.packtpub.com` and apply today. We have worked with thousands of developers and tech professionals, just like you, to help them share their insight with the global tech community. You can make a general application, apply for a specific hot topic that we are recruiting an author for, or submit your own idea.

Table of Contents

Preface

A well-designed cloud infrastructure covers factors such as consistency, maintenance, simplified administration and development, security, scalability, and reusability. Hence, it is important to choose the right architectural pattern as it has a huge impact on the quality of cloud-hosted services.

This book covers all Azure design patterns and functionalities needed to help you build your cloud infrastructure to fit your system requirements. Each of these patterns describes a problem that you normally could have when implementing a cloud infrastructure—a recommended solution for your problem (pattern appliance) and pros and cons of applying this pattern.

Using a pattern (or at least thinking about it) is a recommended way of working when designing an enterprise cloud-based infrastructure.

Who this book is for

This book is targeted at cloud architects and cloud solution providers who are looking for an extensive guide to implementing different patterns for the deployment and maintenance of services in Microsoft Azure. Prior experience with Azure is required as the book is completely focused on design patterns.

What this book covers

Chapter 1, *An Introduction to the Microsoft Azure Platform*, gives an overview of the Azure platform. Also, we will learn the basics of cloud services and cloud deployment models, the Azure execution model, the Azure application building blocks, the Azure data services, and how to access and work with Azure.

Chapter 2, *Compute Design and Management*, discusses the basic architectures behind the compute services from the Azure platform, such as Azure VMs, Azure Container Services, Azure App Services, and Azure Service Fabric. We will also learn that services never act alone, but rather interact with various Azure resources.

Chapter 3, *Data Storing and Processing*, gives basic information on data storage and processing. Here we will get an answer to the question: *How do you choose the right data solution?* We will also see an overview of the Azure data services that are available.

Chapter 4, *Networking Design and Management*, takes you through the anatomy of a VNet, and the network elements also deep dives into connectivity, routing, and more.

Chapter 5, *Availability*, starts with an insight into specific aspects of architecture that are important for the daily use of the Azure platform and are part of the design process for your own Azure solutions.

Chapter 6, *Performance and Scalability*, provides an answer to all your questions related to these topics and also part of the design process for your own Azure solutions.

Chapter 7, *Monitoring and Telemetry*, covers these topics in two parts. In part one, we discuss the question of what type of data we are actually talking about. In part two, we discuss the possible ways to capture this data.

Chapter 8, *Resiliency*, describes the recommended patterns to implement in order to create a cloud-based solution that can handle and recover from failures in a secure way without compromising data and transactions.

Chapter 9, *Identity and Security*, describes the recommended patterns for implementing identity and security features on Azure (for users and for applications and cloud services).

To get the most out of this book

Activate a free Azure subscription (30 days with all the Azure features available to test). Practice with the samples described in the book.

Download the example code files

You can download the example code files for this book from your account at www.packtpub.com. If you purchased this book elsewhere, you can visit www.packtpub.com/support and register to have the files emailed directly to you.

You can download the code files by following these steps:

1. Log in or register at www.packtpub.com.
2. Select the **SUPPORT** tab.
3. Click on **Code Downloads & Errata**.
4. Enter the name of the book in the **Search** box and follow the onscreen instructions.

Once the file is downloaded, please make sure that you unzip or extract the folder using the latest version of:

- WinRAR/7-Zip for Windows
- Zipeg/iZip/UnRarX for Mac
- 7-Zip/PeaZip for Linux

The code bundle for the book is also hosted on GitHub at `https://github.com/PacktPublishing/Implementing-Azure-Cloud-Design-Patterns`. We also have other code bundles from our rich catalog of books and videos available at `https://github.com/PacktPublishing/`. Check them out!

Download the color images

We also provide a PDF file that has color images of the screenshots/diagrams used in this book. You can download it here: `https://www.packtpub.com/sites/default/files/downloads/ImplementingAzureCloudDesignPatterns_ColorImages.pdf`.

Conventions used

There are a number of text conventions used throughout this book.

`CodeInText`: Indicates code words in text, database table names, folder names, filenames, file extensions, pathnames, dummy URLs, user input, and Twitter handles. Here is an example: "Mount the downloaded `WebStorm-10*.dmg` disk image file as another disk in your system."

A block of code is set as follows:

```
public interface IOrderRepository
    {
        List<Order> Read();
        void Write(Order order);
    }
```

When we wish to draw your attention to a particular part of a code block, the relevant lines or items are set in bold:

```
public interface IOrderRepository
    {
        List<Order> Read();
        void Write(Order order);
    }
```

Bold: Indicates a new term, an important word, or words that you see onscreen. For example, words in menus or dialog boxes appear in the text like this. Here is an example: "Now select the **Queues** option and add a new queue"

Warnings or important notes appear like this.

Tips and tricks appear like this.

Get in touch

Feedback from our readers is always welcome.

General feedback: Email `feedback@packtpub.com` and mention the book title in the subject of your message. If you have questions about any aspect of this book, please email us at `questions@packtpub.com`.

Errata: Although we have taken every care to ensure the accuracy of our content, mistakes do happen. If you have found a mistake in this book, we would be grateful if you would report this to us. Please visit `www.packtpub.com/submit-errata`, selecting your book, clicking on the Errata Submission Form link, and entering the details.

Piracy: If you come across any illegal copies of our works in any form on the Internet, we would be grateful if you would provide us with the location address or website name. Please contact us at `copyright@packtpub.com` with a link to the material.

If you are interested in becoming an author: If there is a topic that you have expertise in and you are interested in either writing or contributing to a book, please visit `authors.packtpub.com`.

Reviews

Please leave a review. Once you have read and used this book, why not leave a review on the site that you purchased it from? Potential readers can then see and use your unbiased opinion to make purchase decisions, we at Packt can understand what you think about our products, and our authors can see your feedback on their book. Thank you!

For more information about Packt, please visit `packtpub.com`.

1

An Introduction to the Microsoft Azure Platform

Cloud computing was, and still is, one of the biggest trends in **Information Technology (IT)** in the last 15 years, with many new topics still to be discovered.

At the beginning of this century, most of us didn't use the phrase, cloud computing, but the concept, as well as data centers with massive computing power, was already in existence and being used. Later in that first decade, the word *cloud* became a synonym for nearly anything that was not tangible or online. But the real rise of cloud computing didn't start until the big IT companies (Amazon, Google, and Microsoft) started with their cloud offerings. Now, companies from start-ups to the Fortune 500 are enabled to use cloud services, virtual machines and the like, all with a billing exactly to the minute.

The focus of this book is the Azure platform, which is the cloud offering from Microsoft. In this chapter, I would like to introduce you to the platform, but not in great detail, as over 200 services and 500 updates last year alone cannot be covered in the space we have.

In this chapter, we'll explore the following topics:

- Cloud service models and cloud deployment models
- Azure execution models
- Azure data services
- Azure application blocks
- Azure platform services
- How is Azure access organized?
- How is the work with Azure organized?

Cloud service models and cloud deployment models

Before we start on the actual topic (the Azure platform), we should clarify some terms related to cloud computing. Knowing these concepts, we will then be in a position to identify individual parts of the Azure platform.

Let's start.

Cloud service models

The first term we will look at is **cloud service models**.

All workloads in a cloud scenario use resources from an extremely large resource pool that is operated (managed) by you or a cloud service provider. These resources include servers, storage, networks, applications, services, and much more.

The cloud service models describe to what extent your resources are managed by yourself or by your cloud service providers.

Let's look at the available service models. In the following diagram, you will find a comparison of the models and the existing management responsibilities. Areas that are colored in blue are managed by you: all others are the responsibility of your provider:

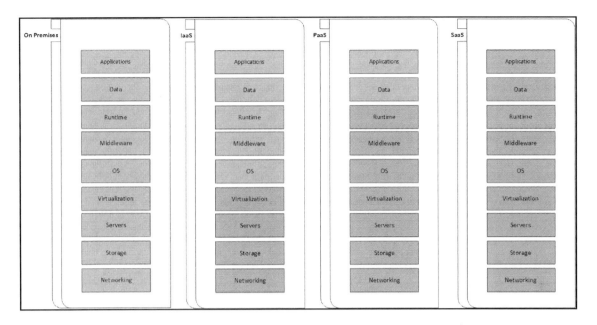

The offers are mainly categorized into the following service models:

- **On-premises**: On-premises describes a model in which the user manages all resources alone.
- **Infrastructure as a Service (IaaS)**: IaaS describes a model in which the cloud provider gives the consumer the ability to create and configure resources from the computing layer upwards. This includes virtual machines, containers, networks, appliances, and many other infrastructure-related resources.
- **Platform as a Service (PaaS)**: PaaS gives the consumer an environment from the operating system upwards. So the consumer is not responsible for the underlying infrastructure.
- **Software as a Service (SaaS)**: SaaS is the model with the lowest levels of control and required management. A SaaS application is reachable from multiple clients and consumers, and the owning consumer doesn't have any control over the backend, except for application-related management tasks.

Cloud deployment models

The second term we will look at is **cloud deployment models**.

Cloud deployment models describe the way in which resources are provided in the cloud.

Which cloud deployment models are available?

Let's look at the following diagram first:

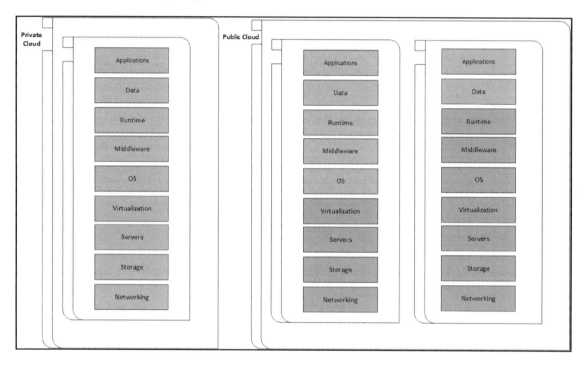

The deployment model based on the on-premises service model is called the **private cloud**. A private cloud is an environment/infrastructure, built and operated by a single organization, which is only for internal use.

In the context of this book, you should know that the Windows Azure Pack (a free add-on for the Windows server) gives you the opportunity to deploy Azure technologies in a private cloud environment.

The deployment model based on the IaaS and the PaaS service model is called the **public cloud**. A public cloud is an offer from a service provider (for example, Microsoft Azure), that can be accessed by the public. This includes individuals as well as companies.

Note: When we talk about Azure in this book, it always means the public cloud model.

There is still a third deployment model available, which is the **hybrid cloud**. A hybrid cloud combines parts of the private and public clouds. It is defined as a private cloud environment at the consumer's site, as well as the public cloud infrastructure that the consumer uses.

In the context of this book, you should know that Azure Stack (a new offering from Microsoft) gives you the opportunity to build a hybrid cloud environment:

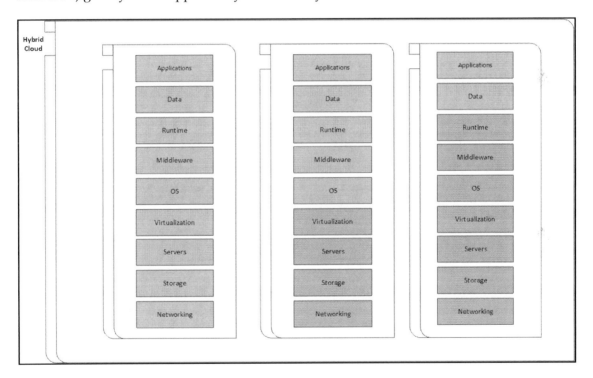

Azure execution models

Now we have acquired some basic knowledge about cloud computing, the question arises: Where do we go Each of these models can be used independently, but also in combination. from here?

I think that when we start talking about the Microsoft Azure platform, we should first talk about running applications in the cloud. For this, Microsoft Azure provides five deployment models (also known as **Azure execution models**), that are outlined in the following diagram:

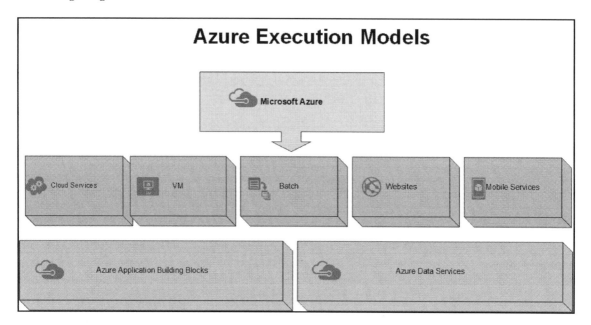

The five execution models are:

- **Cloud services**: Cloud services are the oldest part of the Azure platform and they have been available since its first preview (announced at the Microsoft Professional Developers Conference 2008). Cloud services are a PaaS offering from Azure and even though there are now some alternatives, they are still the leading solution. Cloud services are highly available, scalable, and multi-layered web apps hosted on a Windows Virtual Machine with an installed IIS.
- **Virtual machines** (**VM**): This model is the IaaS offer from Azure. With VMs (based on Windows or Linux OS) you have the flexibility to realize your own workloads. In order to work with VMs as easily as possible, over 3,000 prefabricated images are available in the Azure Marketplace.

- **Batch**: Azure Batch is a platform service for running large-scale parallel and **high performance computing** (**HPC**) applications efficiently in the cloud.
- **Websites**: With this model, you can quickly create and deploy your websites.
- **Mobile services**: With this model, you can quickly create and host a backend for any mobile device.

Each of these models can be used independently, but also in combination.

As I mentioned earlier, there are hundreds of updates every year on the Azure platform and the Azure execution models have also been affected. The execution models' websites and mobile services are now out of date and have been replaced by the execution model, App Services (Azure App Services):

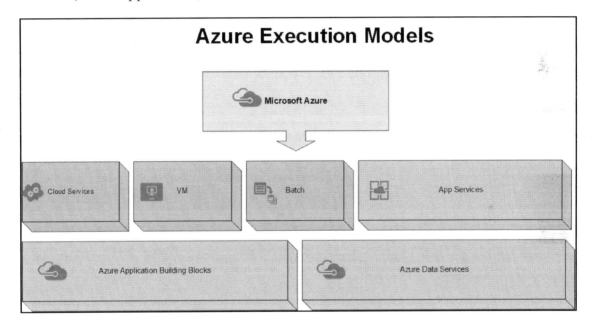

 Azure App Services is not just the replacement for the outdated execution models but much more.

Just look at the following diagram:

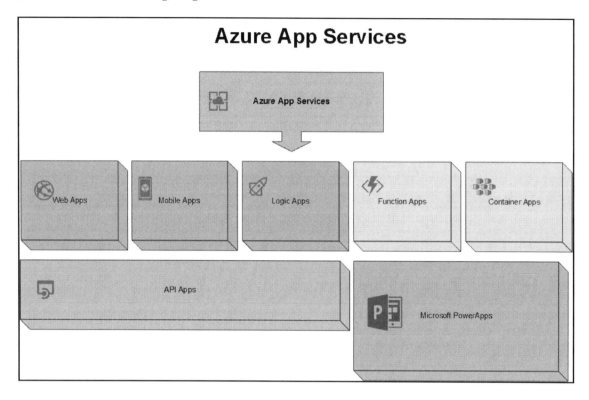

As you can see, the Azure App Services execution model currently consists of the following elements:

- **Web Apps**: Web Apps is simply the new name for the Azure websites' execution model and does not really differ in its functionality from the previous component (by combining it with other app service elements, but there are extended features).
- **Mobile Apps**: Mobile Apps is the new name for the Azure mobile services execution model and does not differ in its functionality from the previous component (by combining it with other app service elements, but there are more features).

- **Logic Apps**: With Logic Apps, you can easily build and deploy powerful integration solutions by automating business processes or integrating your SaaS and enterprise applications. A visual designer is available for creating the necessary workflows. Logic Apps are the next evolutionary step in the Integration Services and the BizTalk services, and starting from 2018 are the only offer in this area.

- **API Apps**: First of all, I must mention that the Azure API Apps are the only truly new component of this model. API Apps allows you to discover, host, manage, and market APIs and SaaS connectors in a modern, feature-rich, scalable, and globally available platform. API Apps is a complete solution for enterprise developers and system integrators, which extends the development of Web Apps (mobile applications) with numerous useful features.

- **Function Apps**: This is not really a component of the Azure App Services. Azure Functions uses the Azure App Services environment only to handle the functionality.

- **Container Apps**: This is not really a component of the Azure App Services. Azure Container Services uses the Azure App Services environment only to handle the functionality.

- **Microsoft PowerApps**: This is not really a component of the Azure App Services. Microsoft PowerApps is a SaaS variant of the Azure App Services and uses the Azure App Services and the Azure App Services environment only to handle the functionality.

A further change to the area of Azure execution models is the addition of another model, Azure Service Fabric (also known as Azure Microservice Architecture), in 2016:

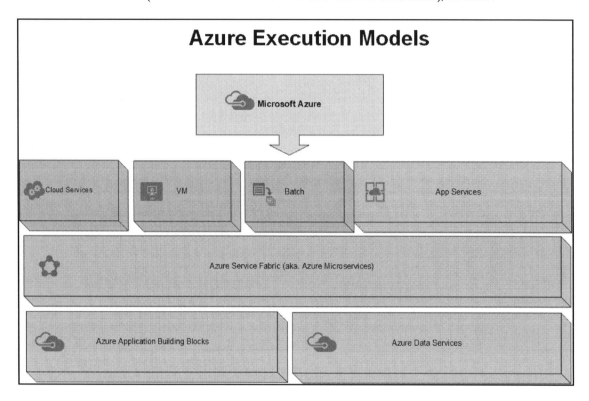

With Azure Service Fabric, you can focus on building applications and business logic, and let the Azure platform solve all other problems by analyzing reliability, scalability, management, and latency.

 More details about Azure Service Fabric and Azure App Services can be found in the next chapter.

Azure application building blocks

Let's return to the last diagram in the previous section. In the bottom layer, you'll find two other components of the Azure platform:

- Azure application building blocks
- Azure data services

Both Azure application building blocks and Azure data services, are managed services that extend the platform with so-called common capabilities (shared functionalities).

In the following diagram, you will find an overview of the Azure application building blocks. Because of the high number of individual components on offer, they are only represented in categories:

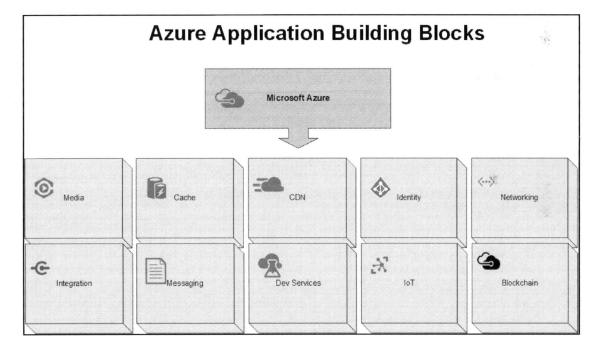

The service categories are as follows:

- **Media**: With the Azure Media Services, the Azure platform provides an extensive portfolio for on-demand and live video processing, video and audio encoding, and much more.
- **Cache**: The use of a cache allows you high throughput and consistent data access with low latency for fast and scalable Azure applications. The solution for the Azure platform called **Azure Redis Cache** is based on the popular open source Redis cache and has been realized as a fully managed service.
- **CDN**: The **Content Delivery Network (CDN)** offers a global solution for delivering high-bandwidth content that is hosted in Azure or any other location (for example any HTTP/HTTPS location).
- **Identity**: This category contains the identity services, such as the Azure **Active Directory (AD)**, Azure AD B2C, Multi-Factor Authentication, and Azure Key Vault which is a safe place for your certificates.
- **Networking**: This category contains the basic networking services. For example, Azure ExpressRoute, VNet Peering, and VPN gateways.
- **Integration**: The integration services include interfaces for hybrid connections, **Enterprise Application Integration (EAI)** and **Electronic Data Interchange (EDI)** message processing, an easy-to-use administrative portal for trading partners as well as support for common EDI schemas and comprehensive EDI processing via X12 and AS2.

> There is an end-of-lifetime message for this area. Existing applications must be upgraded to Azure App Services, Logic Apps and/or to Azure App Services hybrid connections, by June 2018.

- **Messaging**: The messaging services include all interfaces from the Azure Service Bus not included in the integration category, for example, Azure Service Bus topics and Azure Service Bus Notification Hubs.
- **Dev Services**: These are cloud-based development tools for version control, collaboration, and other development-related tasks, for example **Visual Studio Team Services (VSTS)** and the Azure DevTest Labs.
- **IoT**: IoT services include the fundamental tools needed to work with devices used for the IoT, for example Azure IoT Hub, IoT Edge, and Azure Event Hubs.
- **Blockchain**: Blockchain is a way for businesses, industries, and organizations to make and verify transactions—streamlining business processes, and reducing the potential for fraud.

Azure data services

Azure data services are managed services that extend the platform with so-called common capabilities (shared functionalities). Because of the special importance of data in today's digital world, they were separated from the Azure application building blocks and represent a separate kind of service.

In the following diagram, you will find an overview of the Azure data services. Because of the high number of individual components on offer, these are only represented in categories:

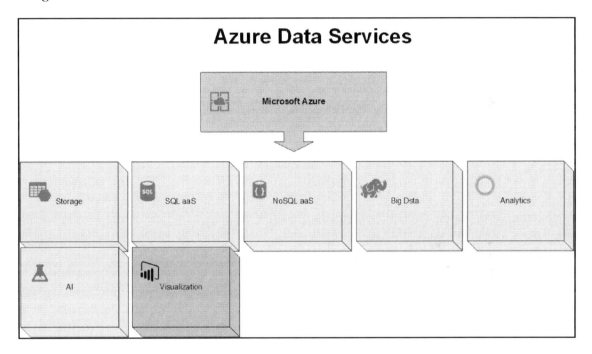

The service categories are as follows:

- **Storage**: This category includes a total of five very different services: Blob Storage (storage of unstructured data), Table Storage (NoSQL storage based on key-value pairs), Queue Storage (for message processing), File Storage, and Disk Storage (Premium Storage).

- **SQL Database as a Service**: This category includes three full managed Databases as a Service: SQL Server, MySQL and PostgreSQL. This category also includes some special offers: SQL Server DWH, SQL Server Stretch DB, SQL Server Elastic DB. All special offers are further developments of the SQL Server as a Service and cover specific cloud workloads.

- **NoSQL Database as a Service**: This category includes a fully managed NoSQL Database as a Service: Azure CosmosDB. A NoSQL database is used to store semi-structured data. A NoSQL database distinguishes between storing key-values, graphs, and document data. You can specify what type of storage you want to use when creating the database.

- **Big Data**: This category includes, along with Azure HDInsight, a fully managed implementation of Apache Hadoop. In addition, implementations (with varying levels of development) are available for Apache Storm, Apache Spark, Apache Kafka, and the Microsoft R Server.

- **Analytics**: This category includes tools to analyze and process data, such as Azure Stream Analytics, Azure Data Lake Analytics, and the Azure Data Factory.

- **AI**: This category includes a fully managed service, **Azure Machine Learning** (**Azure ML**), that enables you to easily build, deploy and share predictive analytics solutions, and also includes some prefabricated solutions for immediate use (Microsoft Cognitive Services).

- **Visualization**: This category is a special case because the offered service (Microsoft PowerBI) is strictly an Azure service but is only offered by Microsoft as an SaaS solution.

Azure platform services

And finally, we now come to a special component of the Azure application building blocks: the Azure platform services. Azure platform services are all services that are responsible for internal workflows on the platform itself.

Since Microsoft has an open strategy for the Azure platform, these services are usually also available to the end user.

Examples of these type of services are as follows:

- Azure Load Balancer
- Azure Traffic Manager and much more

How is access to Azure organized?

In the previous sections of this chapter, we've had an overview of the Azure platform. Now let's dig a bit deeper.

The first point in our discovery journey— How is access to the Azure platform organized?

As long as we look at Azure from our personal point of view, the answer is simple—our entire world consists of an Azure account, a subscription and the direct or indirect handling of Azure resources, as shown here:

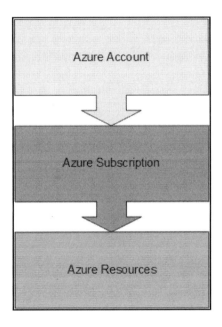

But if we look at the situation from the perspective of an enterprise, it becomes much more complicated, as shown in the next figure. The reason for this is Microsoft's attempt to delineate your company with an Azure enrollment as precisely as possible.

Let's have a look—the high-level element in the figure is now the enterprise element linked to the Enterprise Administrator's role. Here, the most comprehensive and highest rights exist. An Enterprise Administrator is allowed to do everything within the Azure enrollment.

The rights of the Enterprise Administrator include:

- If necessary, he/she can appoint additional Enterprise Administrators
- It defines the so-called departments and appoints corresponding department administrators
- It can set up accounts as required

The Enterprise Administrator is also the only person who can access all consumption and cost data at every level of the Azure enrollment.

The next element is departments (linked to the Department Administrator's role)—with the creation of departments, you can subdivide your enrollment into logical units. Even if the term *department* suggests something different, you have given yourself flexibility in terms of how the elements are divided.

The decision on how elements are classified is actually made based on the following:

- Functional aspects (in fact, according to the organizational structure)
- Business interests (that is according to the project's business)
- Geographical aspects (different locations, branch offices, and so on)

Let's go to the Department Administrators—they have the ability to create accounts within their department and, if necessary, can create a cost center (for a complete cost control).

From the next level, everything is as usual (Azure account, subscriptions, Azure resources and so on):

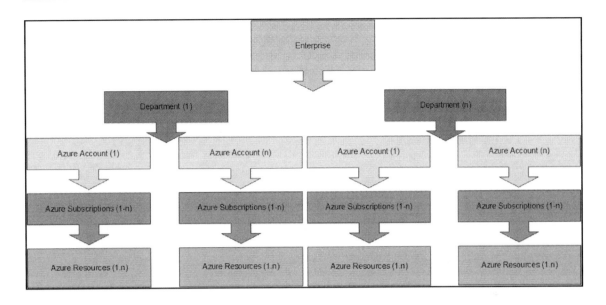

How is work with Azure organized?

Now we know how access to Azure is organized. The question arises— How do I work with Azure?

In general, all work is done through the Azure portal (also known as the Azure management portal).

The Azure portal is a web-based application that can be used to create, manage, and remove all types of Azure resources and services. It includes a customizable dashboard, the ability to create your own dashboards and tooling for managing or monitoring Azure resources. It also provides information for cost and usage management.

The Azure portal is located at `https://portal.azure.com`.

A big thing, but wait, there's even more. Look at the following diagram:

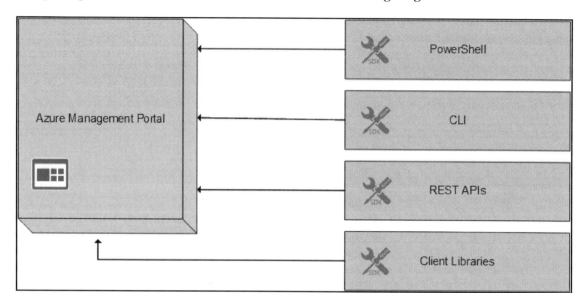

As you can see, there are four other ways to work with Azure, namely:

- **Azure PowerShell**: Azure PowerShell is a set of modules that provides cmdlets to manage Azure. You can use the cmdlets to create, manage, and remove Azure services. In most cases, you can use the cmdlets for the same tasks that you perform in the Azure portal. The cmdlets can help you achieve consistent, repeatable, and hands-off deployments. Azure PowerShell is an open source project and available at `https://github.com/Azure/azure-powershell`.
- **Azure CLI**: The Azure CLI is a tool that you can use to create, manage, and remove Azure resources from the command-line. The Azure CLI is an open source project and available for Linux, macOS, and Windows at `https://github.com/Azure/azure-cli`.
- **REST APIs**: All Azure services, including the Azure management portal, provide their own REST APIs for their functionality. They can therefore be accessed by any application that RESTful services can process.
- **Client libraries**: In order for software developers to write applications in the programming language of their choice, Microsoft offers wrapper classes for the REST APIs. These are available as a so-called Azure SDK for numerous programming languages (for example .NET, Java, Node.js) at `https://github.com/Azure`.

Summary

In this chapter, I've given you an introduction to the Azure platform. You've learned the basics about cloud services and cloud deployment models, had an overview of the Azure execution model, the Azure application building blocks, and the Azure data services, and now know how to access and work with Azure.

In the next chapter, we will start with a more detailed look at the Azure world and you will learn all about the basic architectures behind Azure App Services, Azure Service Fabric, Azure VMs, and Azure Container Services.

2
Compute Design and Management

In the last chapter, I tried to give you a first insight into the Azure platform with a comprehensive introduction. Now, the question arises is how is it going? At least from the viewpoint of the software architect, the question is easy to answer: first, we must make decisions about the technologies used.

OK, now I have to be honest. There is no simple answer. The reasons for this are:

- The large number of available technologies
- The ability to combine offered technologies (typical example: Azure Service Fabric - also known as Azure microservices with Azure Container Services)

But let us return to the keyword decisions now. The decisions that we have to make as a software architect are usually in two areas:

- **Compute**: Compute is the area in which you deploy (host) your applications. This can, for example, be done as an Azure VM, but it is also conceivable within a microservices architecture.
- **Data storing and processing**: This area is quickly explained. No application is today possible without the possibility of storing and, if necessary, processing data. This can, for example, be done by Azure Storage, but also by a more complex solution such as Azure Data Lake.

In this chapter, we will deal with the area *compute* (or at least a selection thereof). However, the selection I made covered at least 90% of all Azure solutions. The area *data storing and processing* follows in the next chapter.

You will learn all about the basic architectures (sometimes also called **architecture styles**) behind the offers. In the places where it is useful, I will also introduce the common design patterns.

In detail, we will explore the following topics in this chapter:

- IaaS I (Azure VMs)
- IaaS II (Azure Container Services)
- PaaS I (Azure App Services)
- PaaS II (Azure Service Fabric, also known as Azure microservices)

IaaS I (Azure VMs)

If you want to run your services within Azure and Microsoft has no **Platform as a Service (PaaS)** or **Software as a Service (SaaS)** offering for that specific service, it is necessary to implement an **Infrastructure as a Service (IaaS)** solution in your environment.

Azure VMs is the IaaS offer from Azure. With VMs (based on Windows or Linux) you have the flexibility to realize your own workloads. These workloads include, in addition to the ability to deploy applications in the cloud, development and testing scenarios and also some enterprise workloads based on Red Hat, Ubuntu, SAP, IBM, and a lot more.

The basic idea behind this offer we now know, but how should we start now? If we look at the whole from the viewpoint of the software architect, the answer is relatively simple: we have to do some planning tasks.

The tasks are as follows:

- Define the workloads for your application and the resources that the VMs need
- Determine the resource requirements for each virtual machine with the appropriate size and storage type of the virtual machines
- Define resource groups for the different levels and components of your infrastructure
- Define a naming convention for your virtual machines and resources (optional, but highly recommended for complex deployments)

For most of this task, I cannot provide any further explanations since they are determined solely by your personal needs within your solution. For the determine resource requirements task, I would like to provide you with some background information.

To complete this task, you should consider the following two questions:

- How many virtual machines do you need for the various application levels of your infrastructure?
- What CPU and memory resources must each VM have and what memory requirements are available?

Question 1, I can unfortunately not answer for you, because the correct answer here also depends on your personal needs. As for question 2, I also cannot give a real answer, but at least I can show you the way you can find a suitable answer for you.

To answer the question for you, you need to know the different sizes and features of the virtual machines. In other words, you have to deal with the VM types.

Since Microsoft supports a broad portfolio of workloads, Microsoft also offers you a wide range of different VM types. Which VM types are available is determined by the so-called Azure series.

What is an Azure series?

The term *Azure series* identifies the available performance levels of an IaaS deployment (provision of a cloud service and/or a VM). The performance levels (that is, the instance) generally differ in the number of CPU cores, the amount of memory, and the maximum size of the data disk.

Some performance levels or even entire Azure series are also defined by special hardware equipment.

Microsoft currently offers the following Azure series:

- **A-series**: The A-series supports the full feature scope of Azure VMs for a wide range of workloads.
- **Basic A**: Light version of the A-series (only available for instances A0-A4). Designed for development and testing starter workloads.
- **A-series (compute intensive)**: High-end version of the A-series. Designed for high-performance computing and data-intensive workloads (for example, video encoding). Optional with high-throughput network interfaces (RDMA).

- **A-series version 2 (Av2-series)**: Av2-series is the latest generation of the A-series and it is specifically designed for Azure DevTest Lab scenarios or for use as an Azure Service Fabric (a microservice architecture). With Av2-series, the performance in data access is significantly higher, since only **Solid State Drives (SSD)** are used for data storage.

- **B-Series**: Series BS is intended for workloads that do not require the full CPU performance continuous, such as web servers, or development and test environments. Each instance of the Series BS provides a basic level (minimum value) for the performance and has then the possibility to extend to a 100% CPU utilization of an Intel® Broadwell E5-2673 v4 2.3GHz or an Intel® Haswell 2.4 GHz E5-2673 v3 processor. As long as you use less than the basic performance with the VM instance, you acquire a credit balance. As soon as your credit has been formed, you can also use the performance that goes beyond the basic level.

All you have to do is answer the question: which basic level best suits my needs? Each instance of the BS Series supports Azure premium storage by default.

- **D-series and DS-series**: D-series VMs are designed to run applications that demand higher compute power and temporary disk performance. To achieve this, a D-series VM provides a better processors performance, a higher memory-to-core ratio, and a SSD are used for the temporary disk.

- **D-series and DS-series version 2 (Dv2-series and DSv2-series)**: Dv2-series and DSv2-series are the next generation of the D-series and DS-series. Dv2-series and DSv2-series are identical to the original series, but have a 35% higher CPU performance based on the Intel Xeon® E5-2673 v3 (Haswell) processor.

- **D-series and DS-series version 3 (Dv3-series and Dsv3-series)**: Dv3-series and Dsv3-series are the latest generation of the D-series and DS-series. Dv3-series and Dsv3-series are based on the Intel® Broadwell E5-2673 v4 2.3 GHz processor, or the Intel® Haswell 2.4 GHz E5-2673 v3 processor and introduce Hyper-Threading Technology and **virtual CPUs (vCPUs)** as key architecture elements. The new series provides also some of the first VM's to be running on a Windows Server 2016 host. Windows 2016 hosts enable nested virtualization and Hyper-V containers for these new instances. Nested virtualization allows you to run a Hyper-V server on an Azure Virtual Machine.

- **Ev3 and ES-series version 3 (Ev3-series and Esv3-series)**: Ev3-series and Esv3-series are also a part from the latest generation of the D-series and DS-series and the new name for the high memory instances D11 - D14. For the Ev3-series and Esv3-series, the same description applies as for the Dv3-series and Dsv3-series.

- **F-series and FS-series**: F-series and FS-series offers a high CPU-to-RAM ratio, ideal for web servers, network appliances, batch processing, and medium-load application servers or real-time communication.
- **FS-series version 2 (Fsv2)**: Fsv2-series are the next generation of the FS-series. The Fsv2-series offers are based on the fastest Intel® Xeon® Scalable processor, code-named Skylake (Intel® Xeon® Platinum 8168 processor), and featuring a base core frequency of 2.7 GHz and a maximum single-core turbo frequency of 3.7 GHz. Fsv2-series provides the Hyper-Threading Technology and the Intel® AVX 512 instructions set, as key architecture elements.
- **G-series and GS-series**: G-series and GS-series are a clone of the older D-series and DS-series, but the G instances have a twice larger memory and four times larger temporary disks based on an SSD. With exceptional high-performance VM sizes in the G range, you can easily handle business critical applications such as large relational database servers (SQL Server, MySQL, and so on) or large NoSQL databases (MongoDB, Cloudera Cassandra, and so on).
- **H-series**: The H-series is designed for high-performance computing and data intensive workloads (for example, molecular modeling and flow dynamics). Optional with high-throughput network interfaces (RDMA).
- **Ls-series**: The Ls-series is a clone from the GS-series and it is built for low latency storage demands above the offerings of GS-series.
- **M-series**: The M-series offers the highest number of CPUs (up to 128 vCPUs) and the largest memory (up to 2.0 TB) for the virtual machine at the Azure platform. This is ideal for extremely large databases or other high end applications that require a high CPU count and large amounts of memory.
- **N-series**: The N-series is not defined by factors such as CPU or memory, but by the possibility to use GPUs (the processors of the graphics card) as an additional power factor. In the form of the GPU, additional computing capacity is provided, whereby the GPU generally operates faster than the CPU in highly parallelizable program sequences (high data parallelism), and therefore, a simple way is sought to supplement the computing performance of CPUs by the computing performance of GPUs. The **Compute Unified Device Architecture** (**CUDA**) and/or **Open Computing Language** (**OpenCL**) technologies are used for this purpose. The use of the GPU performance is particularly suitable for computer- and graphics-intensive workloads and supports you in scenarios such as high-end visualization, deep learning, and predictive analytics.

As you can see, there are some Azure series that have an *s* within the name. Those series VMs use SSDs and Azure premium storage as the primary storage type for data and operating systems. They should be chosen for a regular storage performance over 500 IOPS.

Even if you have decided for an Azure series and a VM type within the planning phase, you can change this decision at any time after deployment.

Is that all? No; in order to work with VMs as easily as possible, there are also over 4,000 prefabricated images available in the Azure Marketplace.

Now, I've been talking about Azure VMs all the time. Nevertheless, the question remains open: what is behind this offer? Since the answer to the question is very complex, I will divide it into several parts. Before I start, however, I have an important note: the following descriptions are valid for all Azure VMs and this is independent from the selected operating system (Linux or Windows). If there are any differences, I will tell you.

Single VMs

Let's start with a single VM and take a look at the first diagram:

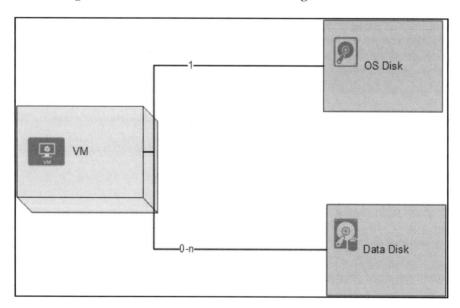

In the preceding diagram, you can see the simplest representation of an Azure VM. An Azure VM consists of an OS disk (which contains the operating system of your VM) and the optional data disks (which serves as a store for the data of your applications). Both disk types are **Virtual Hardware Disks (VHD)** and thus physical files, which are stored as blob in a storage account of your Azure account. The storage of the disks is persistent.

Storage: Microsoft recently added a new option to the Virtual Machines section in Azure. The option is called **Managed Disks**. These disks are abstracted from the classical Azure Storage account and from all storage account limitations. You only have to specify the type, which can be standard or premium storage and the size of the disk you need, and Azure creates and manages the disk for you.

Theoretically, we now have everything together. In reality, however, numerous other resources are still necessary. Some resources are mandatory, other resources can be used as an option.

Let's take a look at the second diagram:

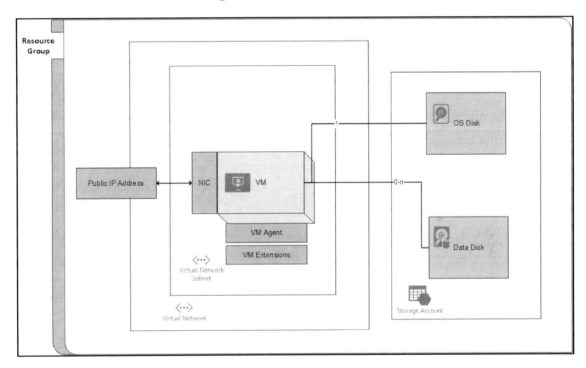

In the preceding diagram, you can now see a complex representation of an Azure VM. Let's look at it once more in detail:

Mandatory resources of an Azure VM are the following:

- **Resource group**: A resource group is a container that holds all related resources
- **Virtual Network (VNet) and VNet subnets**: Every VM in Azure is hosted into a VNet that is supplementarily divided into VNet subnets
- **VM storage account**: The VM storage account is the place where you store the VHDs of the OS disk or the data disks
- **Network interface** (**NIC**): The NIC enables the VM to communicate with the VNet

Optional resources of an Azure VM are the following:

- **VM Agent**: The VM Agent is a lightweight process that manages the VM interaction with the Azure Fabric Controller (this is the main control of the Azure platform). However, the primary role of a VM Agent is to enable and execute Azure VM extensions. The VM Agent is installed by default on any VM deployed from an Azure Gallery image. For VMs based on a custom image, a subsequent manual installation is required.
- **VM extensions**: VM extensions are small applications that provide post-deployment configuration and automation tasks on Azure VMs. The following VM extensions are currently available for the following:
  - **VM Custom Script Extension**: The Custom Script Extension allows any PowerShell script to be run on a virtual machine.
  - **VM PowerShell Desired State Configuration (DSC) extension**: The PowerShell DSC extension allows us to apply PowerShell DSC to a virtual machine.
  - **Operations Management Suite (OMS) Agent extension**: The OMS Agent extensions extends your Azure infrastructure to an OMS workspace.
  - **Azure Log Collector Extension**: The Azure Log Collector enables a log collector to your Azure infrastructure. You can use the extension to perform one-time collection of logs from one or more VMs and transfer the collected files to an Azure Storage account.

- **Azure Diagnostics extensions**: The Azure Diagnostics extension enables Azure Diagnostics to your Azure infrastructure.
- **Microsoft Monitoring Agent VM extension (for Windows only)**: The Microsoft Monitoring Agent VM extension enables Log Analytics to your Azure infrastructure. If you run a Linux VM, use the OMS Agent extension for Linux instead.
- **VM extension for Datadog**: The VM extension for Datadog extends your Azure infrastructure to a Datadog environment (extended monitoring).
- **VM extension for Chef**: The VM extension for Chef extends your Azure infrastructure to a Chef environment (extended monitoring and configuration).
- **Public IP address**: A public IP address is needed to communicate with the VM-for example over the **Remote Desktop Service (RDP)**.

Not shown in the diagram is the following resource (also optional):

- **Network Security Group (NSG)**: An NSG is used to allow or deny network traffic. You can associate an NSG with an individual NIC or with a VNet subnet. If you associate it with a VNet subnet, the NSG rules apply to all VMs in that subnet.

Multiple VMs

Now you've learned everything about deploying of a single VM, but in real life, usually there is more than only one VM instance. In principle, you need to provide the same Azure resources for several VM instances, as when deploying only one. Nevertheless, there are differences and I will now explain them.

Take a look at the following diagram:

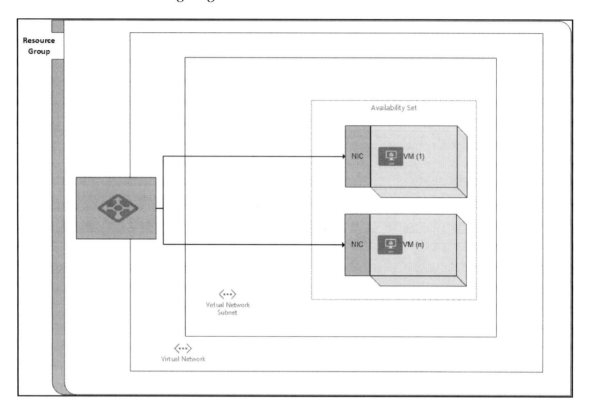

We start with the most important innovation in this representation.

Azure availability sets

The available sets are an organization component (resource) of the Azure platform and they manage the operation of two or more instances of a VM. The available sets ensure that the VM instances are always running on different fault and update domains of the Azure platform, so that at least one instance is always online.

Fault Domain: Fault domain in Azure means that all servers in these domains run in the same fire sections, with the same air condition or electrical source which means all physical servers within in those domains, can have an outage at the same time.

Update domain: Update domain in Azure means that all physical servers in an update domain will get updates like firmware, drivers, and OS updates at the same time.

Let's look at the next novelty in this view: if you look closely, you can see here an instance of the Azure Load Balancer which serves as an entry point to the architecture. The load balancer has the task to forward incoming internet requests to the provided VMs.

The load balancer requires the following additional resources to perform its tasks:

- **Public IP address**: A public IP address is needed for the load balancer to receive internet traffic
- **Frontend configuration**: Associates the public IP address with the load balancer
- **Backend address pool**: It contains the NICs for the VMs that will receive the incoming traffic

Not shown in the diagram are the following resources:

- **Load balancer rules**: Load balancer rules are used to distribute network traffic among all the VMs in the backend address pool.
- **Network address translation (NAT) rules**: NAT rules are used to route traffic to a specific VM. But beware, if you want to enable, for example, the RDP for the VMs, you must create a separate NAT rule for each VM.

N-tier deployment

Now we know all the basics and it is time to make a complex architecture (N-tier architecture) out of this.

Let's take a look at the following diagram:

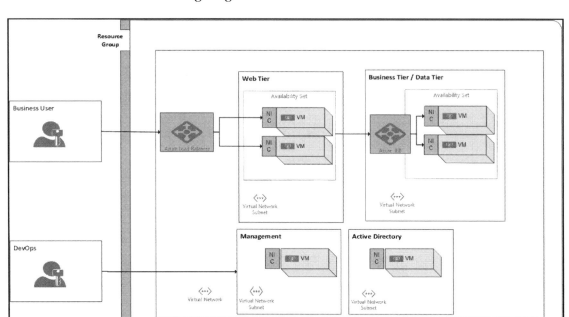

What is different here? The architecture is again based on the pattern for multiple VMs, but this time, the design is repeated several times because the architecture is divided into at least the following three levels:

- Web tier or frontend application
- Business tier or business logic
- Data tier

Not required, but nevertheless often present, are the following levels:

- Management tier
- Active Directory

All actually existing levels within this architecture are also single subnets of the VNet.

The entry point for this architecture is again the Azure Load Balancer, which is only used to distribute incoming internet traffic to the web tier, the Azure **Internal Load Balancer (ILB)** is then used for all other levels.

 Unlike the Azure Load Balancer, the ILB requires a private IP address. To give the ILB a private IP address, create a frontend IP configuration and associate it with the subnet for the business tier.

Let's go back to distribution from incoming internet traffic. Not visible, but still present, are the numerous **network security groups** (**NSGs**) that are respectively associated with the subnet. An NSG is used to regulate network traffic by allowing or denying network traffic. For our architecture, this means, for example, that you can use the help of an NSG to decide that the data from the web tier can only be passed on to the business tier.

Now, I have some additional information about the optional architectural layers:

- **Management tier (also known as jumpbox or bastion host)**: The Management tier includes a secure VM on the network that administrators (or DevOps) use to connect to the other VMs. Note that the most of the time the management tier has an NSG that allows remote traffic only from public IP addresses on a safe list. The NSG should also permit the use of the RDP. The management tier is also a good place to install a monitoring solution such as Nagios or Zabbix that can give you an insight into response time, VM uptime, and the overall health of your system.
- **Active Directory Tier**: The Active Directory tier includes a VM with installed **Active Directory Domain Service** (**AD DS**). An Active Directory tier is only required if you use an SQL Server Always-On Availability Group as Data tier. Prior to Windows Server 2016, SQL Server Always-On Availability Groups must be joined to a domain. This is because availability groups depend on the **Windows Server Failover Cluster** (**WSFC**) technology. Windows Server 2016 provides the ability to create a failover cluster without Active Directory. If your architecture is based on Windows Server 2016, the AD DS server is not required.

N-tier (multi-regions) deployment

In conclusion, I would like to present you with a variant of N-tier architecture: N-tier multi-regions. This variant is designed for high availability and as a disaster recovery infrastructure. Let's take a look at the following diagram:

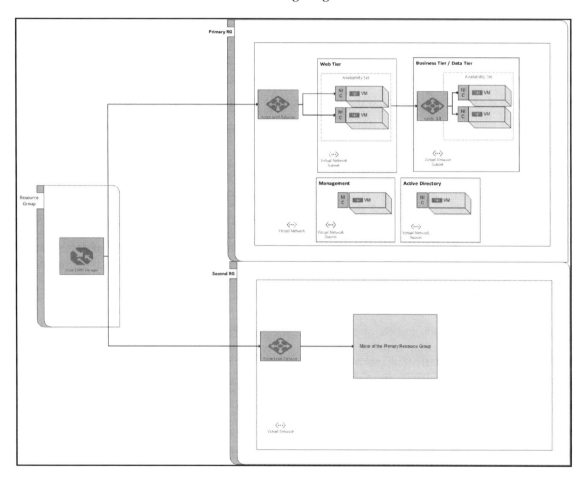

What is different here? The architecture shown here is divided into three resource groups. Two resource groups (located in two Azure regions) are based on the already presented N-tier architecture and are thus identical. One of these resource groups is called the primary resource group and is for daily use. The other resource group (called the secondary resource group) serves as a failover.

The third resource group only includes an instance of the Azure Traffic Manager as a resource. The Azure Traffic Manager is the new entry point for this architecture and routes incoming requests to one of the regions. During normal operations, it routes requests to the primary resource group. If that region becomes unavailable, the traffic manager fails over to the secondary resource group.

There is another difference in the primary resource group and the secondary resource group —an additional subnet was added, which includes a VPN gateway. With the VPN gateway, you can configure a VNet-to-VNet connection, to enable network traffic between the two VNets.

IaaS II (Azure Container Services)

Azure Container Services are a new variant of the classical Azure IaaS offer from Azure (descripted in the first section of this chapter), and they also use virtual machines as the technological base.

Two versions of the Azure IaaS are offered, and both are based on virtual machines, but Azure Container Services has some advantages over the older solution due to its additional functionality.

I will now take a closer look at these advantages and introduce Azure Container Services in detail.

What is an Azure Container Service?

An Azure Container Service helps you to create, configure, or manage a cluster of VMs. These clusters are preconfigured to run applications in so-called **containers**.

OK; this is a complete answer, but we should nevertheless take a deeper look.

Let's start with a comparison between the two Azure IaaS offers. The following diagram shows you the classic Azure IaaS offer, or in other words, Windows or Linux VMs on Azure:

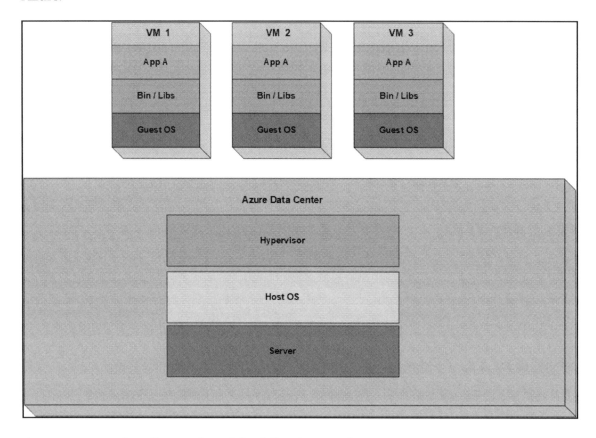

As you can see, the offer consists of the following two layers:

- The infrastructure in Azure data center
- The actual VMs

The area infrastructure is easily explained; VMs are an abstraction of physical hardware running on a server and turn one server into many servers. The hypervisor allows you to run several VMs on a single machine.

Now we come to the area VMs, each VM includes one or more apps, the necessary libraries and binaries, and a full guest operating system.

A VM can reach a size in the high GB range and can therefore be very slow when booting.

The following diagram shows you the new Azure IaaS offer, or in other words, the IaaS based on a container solution:

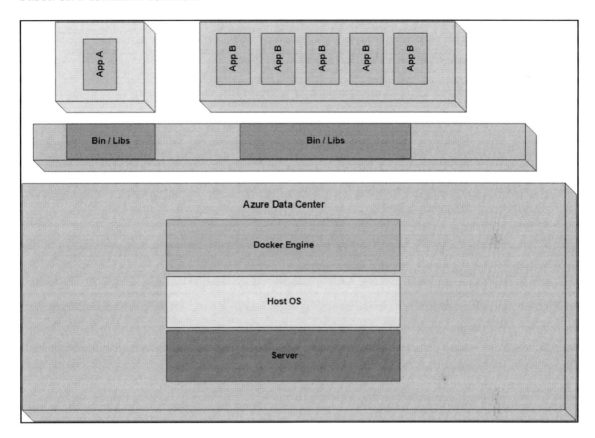

At first glance, this diagram looks like the first diagram. But there are some differences.

In the infrastructure layer, for example, you will find a container engine instead of the hypervisor. In Azure Container Service, the container engine is a **Docker Engine**. Docker is currently the leading open source project for container solutions.

 In good Azure tradition, the Azure Container Service engine is an open source project. If you want to examine the engine internals, or if you need to adjust your needs, you can find the complete source code at https://github.com/Azure/acs-engine.

Let's come back to the subject. The container engine is the runtime environment for containers (partially comparable to the guest OS of the VMs). With their help, multiple containers can run on the same machine and share the OS kernel with other containers that run as isolated processes in their own user space.

The next difference in the new offer, you will find in the provision of the necessary libraries and binaries. They are provided by the container engine in an intermediate layer for individuals or as a shared resource for multiple containers.

Understanding containers

The term has already been mentioned several times, so it is time to ask: what is a container? There is a simple answer, a container in our mind is an instance of a Docker image. A Docker image is an ordered collection of root filesystem changes and the corresponding execution parameters.

When you scale your Azure Container Service, you typically run multiple containers from the same image.

A container is defined not only by a Docker image, but also by the following components:

- A so-called Dockerfile is a text file that contains necessary information about the structure of the container
- Something singular like a process, a service, or microservice (for example, an Azure Service Fabric) or an app

Containers take up less space than VMs (typically in a low MB range), and start almost instantly.

Now we have gained our first insights into the container issue. To understand the following, however, we must clarify a few more terms.

Cluster

The first term is **cluster** or **Docker cluster**. A cluster bundles several Docker hosts and represents them as a single virtual host. A cluster is thus able to scale very easily and this with an unlimited number of hosts.

Why do I tell you this? There is a simple answer, when we are speaking about the creation of an Azure Container Service, it means the creation of a cluster and not the creation of a container application.

Orchestrator

The next term is **Orchestrator**. An Orchestrator is a management tool for Docker clusters and Docker hosts, and it enables users to manage their images, containers, and hosts through a GUI.

The Orchestrator allows users to administer container networking, configurations, load balancing, service discovery, high availability, host management, and is responsible for running, distributing, scaling, and healing workloads across a collection of nodes.

When you create your Azure Container Service cluster, you also decide about the Orchestrator you want to use.

The following Orchestrators are currently available:

- DC/OS
- Kubernetes
- Docker Swarm

Which Orchestrator should I choose?

Microsoft does not recommend a specific Orchestrator. If you have experience with one of the Orchestrators, you can continue to use this experience in Azure Container Service.

However, there are trends that indicate that **Datacenter Operating System (DC/OS)** is good for big data and IoT workloads. Kubernetes is suitable for cloud-native workloads and Docker Swarm is known for its integration with other Docker tools and for its easy learning curve. Let's take a deeper look at the three Orchestrators.

Mesosphere DC/OS

Mesosphere DC/OS is a distributed operating system based on the Apache Mesos distributed systems kernel.

DC/OS and Apache Mesos include the following features:

- Scalability
- Fault-tolerant replicated master and slaves using Apache ZooKeeper
- Support for Docker containers
- Native isolation between tasks with Linux containers
- Scheduling for multiple resources (memory, CPU, disk, and ports)

- Java, Python, and C++ APIs
- A web UI for viewing cluster state (Apache Mesos UI)

By default, DC/OS includes the marathon orchestration platform for scheduling workloads and Mesosphere universe, a collection of services that can be added to your service.

The following diagram shows the architecture of an Azure Container Service cluster using DC/OS:

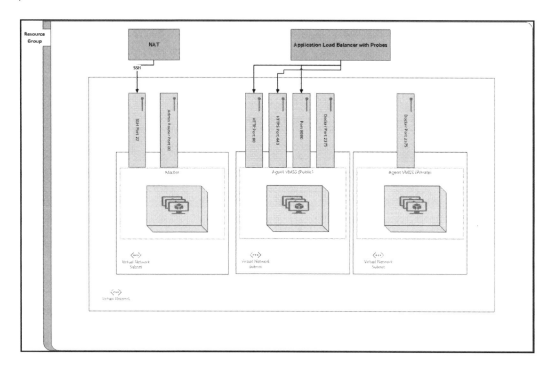

For further information on Mesosphere DC/OS please visit https://dcos.io/. You can find the complete source code at https://github.com/dcos.

Docker Swarm

Docker Swarm offers a system-specific clustering feature for Docker. Because Docker handles Docker Swarm's standard API, any tool that already communicates with a Docker daemon can use Swarm.

Supported tools for the managing of containers on a Swarm cluster are:

- Dokku (an ALM tool)
- Docker CLI
- Docker compose
- Jenkins

The following diagram shows the architecture of an Azure Container Service cluster using Docker Swarm:

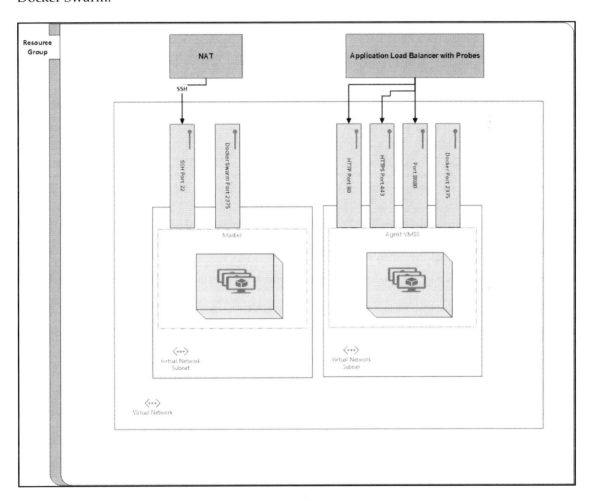

For further information on Docker Swarm, please visit `https://www.docker.com/`. The complete source code you can find at `https://github.com/docker`.

Kubernetes

Kubernetes is a popular production-grade container Orchestrator tool. Kubernetes automates deployment, scaling, and management of containerized applications.

Kubernetes includes the following features:

- Horizontal scaling
- Service discovery and load balancing
- Secrets and configuration management
- API-based automated rollouts and rollbacks
- Self-healing

The following diagram shows the architecture of an Azure Container Service cluster using Kubernetes:

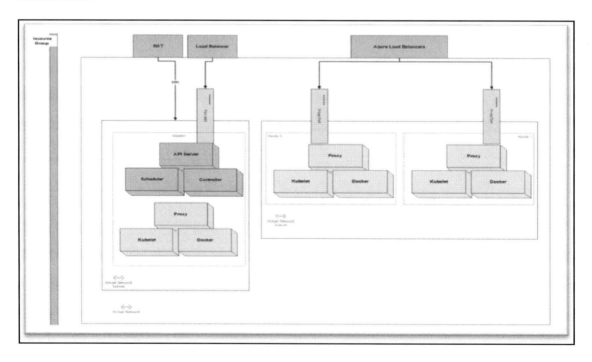

For further information on Kubernetes please visit `https://kubernetes.io/`. The complete source code you can find at `https://github.com/kubernetes`. All three Orchestrators are open source projects with frequent version changes. These version changes are considered by Azure Container Service, but unfortunately there is currently no possibility to upgrade an existing deployment.

PaaS I (Azure App Services)

In the last two sections of this chapter, I have given you the most important facts about the offers in the area Azure IaaS. Now, we are leaving this area in the direction of the PaaS area.

What is a PaaS solution? A PaaS solution is a service or a complete service environment that allows you to deploy and run your own applications.

Let's go to the actual subject of this section: the Azure App Services. Azure App Services are defined as a service environment and are also a part of the Azure Execution Models.

Let's take a look at the first diagram:

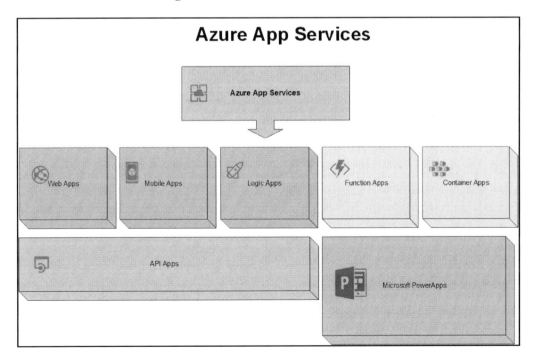

As you can see, the Azure App Services currently consists of the following elements:

- **Web Apps**: Web apps is simply the new name for the Azure websites execution model and does not really differ in its functionality from the previous component (by combining it with other app service elements, but there are extended possibilities).
- **Mobile Apps**: Mobile apps is the new name for the Azure Mobile Services execution model and does not differ in its functionality from the previous component (by combining it with other app service elements, but there are more possibilities).
- **Logic Apps**: With Logic Apps, you can easily build and deploy powerful integration solutions by automating business processes or integrating your SaaS and enterprise applications. A visual designer is available for creating the necessary workflows. Logic Apps are the next evolutionary step in the integration services and the BizTalk services and starting from 2018 they are only offered in this area.
- **API Apps**: First of all, I must have mentioned that the Azure API apps are the only truly new component of this model. API apps allows you to discover, host, manage, and market APIs and SaaS connectors in a modern, feature-rich, scalable, and globally available platform. API apps is a complete solution for enterprise developers and system integrators, which extends the development of web apps (mobile apps) with numerous useful features.
- **Function App**: Not really a component of the Azure App Services. Azure Functions uses the Azure App Services environment only to handle the functionality.
- **Container Apps**: Not really a component of the Azure App Services. Azure Container Services uses the Azure App Services environment only to handle the functionality.
- **Microsoft PowerApps**: Not really a component of the Azure App Services. Microsoft PowerApps is a SaaS variant of the Azure App Services and uses the Azure App Services technologies and the Azure App Services environment only to handle the functionality.

Now, we have a first overview, but to get a deeper insight, we should change the diagram somewhat. Attention: in this diagram, some elements (for example, Function apps) have been removed because they only fit to a limited extent in the overall concept:

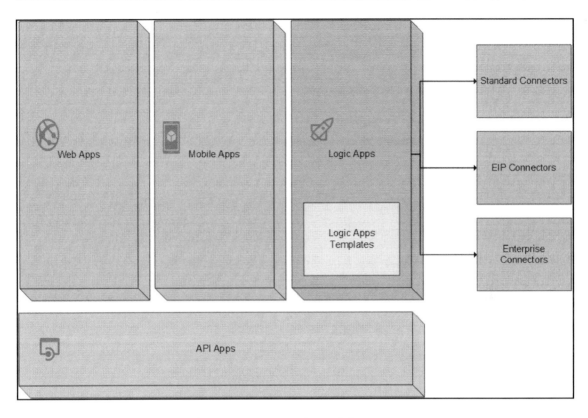

Our image of the Azure App Services now consists of three areas:

- Frontend
- Logic
- API

The frontend area includes:

- **Web Apps**: Web apps are all kinds of websites and web applications based on ASP.NET, Node.js, Java, PHP, and Python
- **Mobile Apps**: Mobile apps gives you the ability to develop apps regardless of whether you want to create native iOS, Android, and Windows apps, or cross-platform Xamarin or Cordova apps (PhoneGap).

The Logic area includes:

- **Logic Apps**: Logic Apps enable the simple implementation of scalable integrations and workflows into the cloud. For this, a visual designer is provided with which you can model and automate your processes in the form of a workflow. Other components of the Azure Logic Apps are the Logic App Templates and the Connectors.
- **Logic App Templates**: A Logic app template is a pre-built logic app that serves as the starting point for creating your own workflows.
- **Connectors**: Connectors are the most important part of an Azure logic app. With the usage of these connectors, you can expand your on-premises or cloud applications to do different things with data that you create, or data you already have. The connectors are available in the following categories:
  - **Standard Connectors**: Standard connectors are out-of-the-box connectors and are automatically available and included when you use Azure Logic Apps. Some examples are:
    - Azure Service Bus
    - Azure Blob storage
    - Azure Functions
    - Microsoft Power BI
    - Twitter and many more
  - **Protocol Connectors**: Protocol connectors are a part of the standard connectors and include four examples:
    - HTTP
    - HTTP and Swagger
    - HTTP WebHook
    - Request/response (HTTPS)
  - **EIP Connectors**: EIP connectors are also known as **integration account connectors**: EIP connectors are available when you install the enterprise integration pack and create an integration account. Using these connectors, you can transform and validate XML, process business-to-business messages with AS2/X12/EDIFACT, and encode and decode flat files. These connectors are also good to expand BizTalk workflows into Azure.

Additional costs are associated with the use of the EIP connectors.

- **Enterprise Connectors**: With Enterprise connectors, you can connect your Azure Logic Apps within your enterprise applications. This category includes three examples:
  - IBM MQ server
  - SAP application server
  - SAP Message Server

Some connectors can also act as a trigger. A trigger starts a new instance of an Azure Logic App workflow based on a specific event, like a change in your Azure Storage account.

The following triggers are available:

- **Poll triggers**: These triggers poll your service at a specified frequency to check for new data. When new data is available, a new instance of your logic app runs with the data as input.
- **Push triggers**: These triggers listen for data on an endpoint, or for an event, and then triggers a new instance of your logic app.
- **Recurrence trigger**: This trigger instantiates an instance of your logic app on a prescribed schedule.

The API area includes:

- **API apps**: API apps give you the opportunity to host your own APIs in all supported programming languages (ASP.NET, C #, Java, PHP, Node.js, and Python). API apps provides support for the OpenAPI (Swagger) Metadata API and is, for example, a great way to create a custom connector for an Azure Logic App.

Now, we have won a deeper insight, and we should take a look at a typical basic architecture:

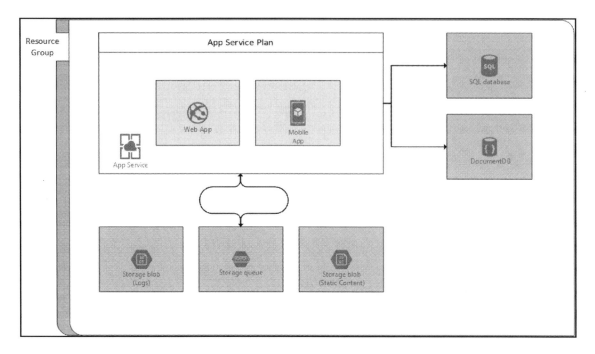

The architecture is relatively simple to explain:

You always have a resource group with the following required elements:

- One App Service plan
- One or more web apps and/or mobile apps

In addition, there are at least two storage accounts based on the storage blob service for:

- Log files (application logs or diagnostics logs)
- Static content (for example, images)

The following elements are optional:

- A storage account based on the storage queue service
- A SQL Database as a service solution like Azure SQL service and/or a NoSQL database as a service solution such as Azure Cosmos DB (formerly Azure DocumentDB)

Which of these optional elements is actually used depends on your individual scenarios.

Let's return to the phrase App Service plans, an App Service plan represents a collection of physical resources that are used to host your apps.

An App Service plan defines:

- Region (for example, North Europe)
- Scaling (number of instances)
- Instance size (small, medium, large)
- SKU (Free, Shared, Basic, Standard, Premium. Premium V2, Isolated)

 An App Service Plan is also an Azure VM. The actual performance of your ASP depends also on the selected Azure series.

In the SKUs, Premium, Premium V. 2.0, and Isolated is a special feature included, which we should explain:

Azure **App Service Environment** (**ASE**): An ASE is a feature that provides a fully isolated and dedicated environment for securely running all types of App Service apps at high scale.

An ASE is always created inside of a virtual network and more precisely, within a subnet of a virtual network. This enables apps to securely connect to other endpoints accessible only inside of a virtual network, including endpoints connected via Azure Site-to-Site or Azure ExpressRoute connections.

There are two deployment types for an ASE:

- **External ASE**: An External ASE exposes the hosted apps on an internet-accessible IP address.

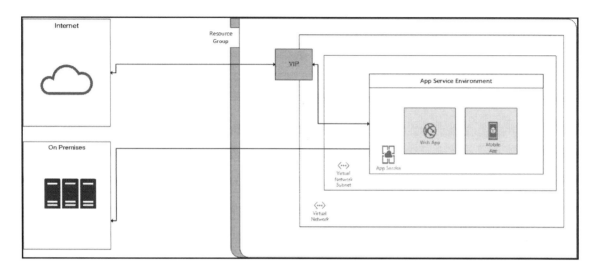

- **Internal load balancer (ILB) ASE**: An ILB ASE exposes the hosted apps on an IP address inside your VNet. The endpoint in this case is an instance of the Azure ILB.

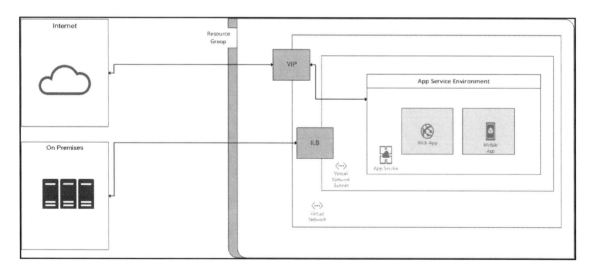

Apps running in an ASE also have even more scaling options, including the ability to run on up to 100 compute instances.

Is that all? There is a clear answer: no. Recently, the Azure App Services portfolio has been extended by two other offerings:

- Azure App Service on Linux
- Azure Web Apps for Containers

With the Azure App Service on Linux offer you now have the option to run .NET Core, Node.js, PHP, or Ruby applications natively on a Linux VM inside from Azure App Service.

 The underlying architecture and the applications themselves are container applications (built-in Docker images).

Let's go to the second new offer, the Azure Web App for Containers. Again, this is about applications (container applications) running natively on a Linux VM. The difference between the two offers is with the Docker images used. While the Azure App Service on Linux option uses ready-made built-in images, the Azure Web Apps for Containers use so-called **custom images**. So, you have direct control over which packages are installed, which runtime frameworks are used, or which tooling is available.

PaaS II (Azure Service Fabric, also known as Azure microservices)

Azure Service Fabric is a PaaS offer for distributed systems that simplifies the packing, provisioning, and management of scalable and reliable microservices. Before we start with a deep analysis, we should deal with the microservice architecture in general.

Let's take a look at the first diagram:

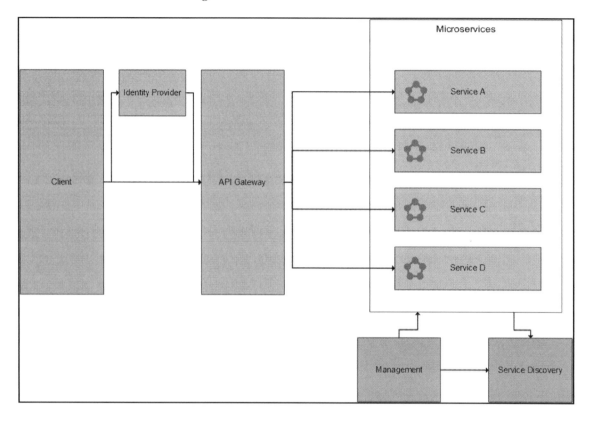

Core elements of this architecture are the services (or microservices). The services are defined by the following characteristics:

- A service is small, which means a service offers only one function in contrast to the application with many functions.
- A service is independent. This has several meanings for our work:
    - Each service has a separate code base, and this without the need to share the same technology stack, libraries, or frameworks. You can use, for example, C# for the first, Java for the second, and a JavaScript framework for the third service
    - Each service can be managed or deployed from a separate development team or a business unit, and this without the need to rebuild or redeploy an entire application in the case of updating an existing service.

- Each service is responsible for persisting their own data or external state. This is a big difference from the traditional model, where a separate data layer handles data persistence.
- Services are loosely coupled. Imagine the microservice architecture as a pool of work units. You can call up at any time a single work unit to work on a specific task or to implement any combination of work units to perform complex tasks:
  - Services communicate with each other by using a well-defined API. Internal implementation details of each service are hidden from other services.

The other elements of the architecture are:

- API gateway. The API gateway is the entry point for the microservice architecture because a typical client never calls a service directly. Instead, the client calls the API gateway, which forwards the call to the corresponding services on the backend.
- Another operational scenario for the use of the API gateway is, you can summarize the answers of multiple services and then return the aggregated response.

In general, the advantages of using an API gateway are the following:

- It decouples clients from services. This allows services to be versioned or redesigned without the need to update all clients.
- Services can use messaging protocols that are not available on the internet, for example AMQP.
- The API Gateway can also perform other tasks. For example, authentication, logging, or load balancing.

Management: The management component is responsible for the placement of services on the node, the identification of errors, the realignment of services across nodes, and so on.

Service Discovery: The service discovery component includes a list of services and a description on which nodes they are located. This enables a service lookup to find the endpoint for a specific service.

Now we have an idea of how a microservice architecture looks in general. Next, we should look at the whole from the view of Microsoft Azure.

In other words, we should now clarify what is behind the Azure Service Fabric offer.

We begin with a general answer: Azure Service Fabric provides you with a simple solution to the complex challenges of developing and managing cloud applications. You can avoid infrastructure issues and focus on implementing business-critical workloads that are scalable, reliable, and easy to manage.

Now let's go a step further into the details. Look at the following diagram, with information about the Azure Service Fabric infrastructure:

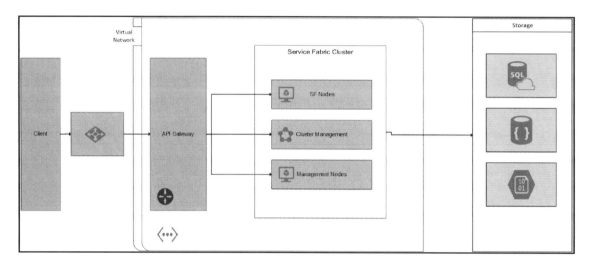

The key element of the infrastructure is the **Service Fabric Cluster**. A cluster contains a network-connected set of virtual or physical computers on which your microservices are deployed and managed. Clusters can be scaled to thousands of computers.

A computer or a virtual computer that is part of a cluster is referred to as a node. Each node receives a node name. Nodes have features such as placement properties.

Some nodes have administrative tasks, for example, for error monitoring. These nodes are then called **management nodes**.

Not shown in the diagram, but still present:

- Each computer or virtual machine has a Windows startup (FabricHost.exe) service that runs on startup and starts two executable files: Fabric.exe and FabricGateway.exe. These two executable files together form the nodes.
- In a development environment, you can host multiple nodes on a single computer or virtual machine by running multiple instances of Fabric.exe and FabricGateway.exe.

Let's take a closer look at the Azure Service Fabric offer:

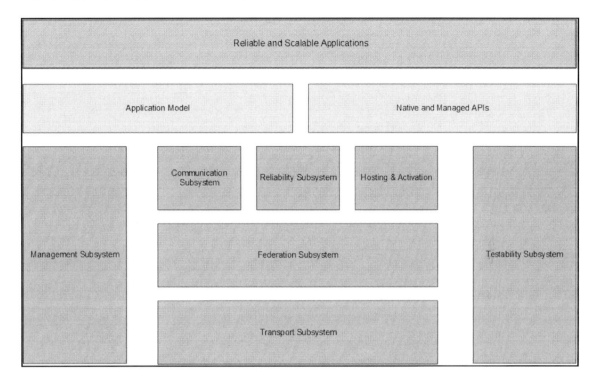

- **Programming models**: Azure Service Fabric offers you various options to develop your services. You can use the offered Service Fabric APIs to access the platform's full set of functions, or you can write your services in any programming language, and then host the service on a service fabric cluster. The Azure Service Fabric provides the following offers and concepts for developers:
    - **Guest executables**: A so-called guest executable is an arbitrary executable that can be run as a part of your application. This type of executable never calls the Service Fabric APIs directly, but they still use all features the platform offers by calling the REST APIs provided from the Service Fabric.

- **Reliable services**: Reliable services is a framework for developing services that provide a full integration in the Service Fabric platform and make use from the full set of platform features. The framework provides you with a set of APIs that allow the Service Fabric runtime to manage the life cycle of your services and that allow your services to interact with the runtime. The framework also gives you full control over design and implementation choices, and you can use it to host any other application framework, such as ASP.NET Core. Reliable services can be stateless, similar to most service platforms, in which each instance of the service is created equal and state is persisted in an external solution, such as Azure Cosmos DB or Azure Table Storage. Reliable services can also be stateful, where the state is persisted directly in the service itself using so-called **reliable collections**. The state is made highly-available through replication and is distributed through partitioning.

- **Reliable actors**: The reliable actor framework (built on top of the reliable services framework) is a framework that implements the virtual actor pattern, based on the actor design pattern. The reliable actor framework uses independent units of compute and state with single-threaded execution called actors. The reliable actor framework provides a built-in communication for actors and pre-set state persistence and scale-out configurations. Like the reliable services framework, the reliable actor framework is fully integrated into the service fabric platform and uses the complete function set offered by the platform.

- **ASP.NET Core**: The Service Fabric platform also provides integration with ASP.NET Core for building web and API services that can be included as part of your services.

- **Management subsystem**: The management subsystem handles the life cycle of applications and services. For this the subsystem provides the following tools:

  - **Cluster manager**: The cluster manager is the primary service that interacts with the failover manager from the reliability subsystem to place the applications on the nodes according to the restrictions on service placement. The resource manager in the failover subsystem then ensures that these constraints are always respected. The cluster manager also manages the life cycle of the applications from provision to de-provision, and is integrated with the health manager to ensure that application availability is not lost from a health perspective during upgrades.

- **Health manager**: The health manager allows you to monitor the integrity of applications, services, and cluster entities (for example, nodes, service partitions, or replicas). Cluster entities can report status information that is then aggregated to the central health store. This integrity information provides a snapshot of the integrity of each service and each node that are distributed across the cluster. You can use this information to make necessary corrective action. Integrity query APIs are used to query integrity events reported to the integrity subsystem. The integrity query APIs return the raw integrity data stored in the integrity store or the aggregated, interpreted integrity data for a particular cluster entity.
- **Image store**: The image store provides storage and distribution for the application binaries. The image store is offered in the form of a simple distributed file store, where the applications are uploaded and downloaded.

- **Communication subsystem**: The communication subsystem provides reliable messaging within the cluster through the so-called **naming service**. The naming service resolves service names to a location in the cluster and enables users to also manage service names and properties.
- **Reliability subsystem**: The reliability subsystem provides the mechanism to make the state of a Service Fabric service highly available. For this the subsystem provides the following tools:
    - **Replicator**: The replicator ensures that state changes in secondary replicas are automatically replicated by state changes in the primary service replica. The replicator saves the consistency between the primary and secondary replicas in a so-called service replica set. Fabric replicator makes the service state highly available and reliable.
    - **Failover manager**: The failover manager ensures that when nodes are added to or removed from the cluster, the load is automatically redistributed across the available nodes. If a node in the cluster fails, the cluster will automatically reconfigure the service replicas to maintain availability.
    - **Resource manager**: The resource manager places replicas of your services over the failure domain in the cluster and ensures that all failover units are operational. The resource manager also balances service resources across the underlying shared pool of cluster nodes to achieve optimal load distribution.

- **Hosting subsystem**: The cluster manager (part of the management subsystem) informs the hosting subsystem (running on each node of the cluster) which services it needs to manage for a particular node. The subsystem then manages the life cycle of this specific service on this node. The subsystem also interacts with the reliability and health components to ensure that the replicas are properly placed and are healthy.

- **Federation subsystem**: In order to assess the importance of a group of nodes in a distributed system, you must understand the entire system as a whole. The federation subsystem uses the communication functions provided by the transport subsystem and merges the various nodes into a single unified cluster that is viewed as a whole. It provides the master functions of the distributed system required by the other subsystems, for example, error detection, leader election, and consistent forwarding. The subsystem builds on distributed hash tables with a 128-bit token span. The subsystem creates a ring topology. The federation subsystem also guarantees through intricate join and departure protocols that only a single owner of a token exists at any time. For error detection, the subsystem uses a leasing mechanism that is based on monitoring heartbeats and switching. The federated subsystem also ensures that only one user can be owned by the token at a time with complex access and exit protocols. This is, for example, the prerequisite for guaranteeing consistent forwarding.

- **Transport subsystem**: The transport subsystem implements a point-to-point communication channel, and this channel is then used for communication within service fabric clusters and communication between the service fabric cluster and clients. It supports one-way and request-response communication patterns, which provides the basis for implementing broadcast and multicast in the federation subsystem. The transport subsystem secures the communication by using X509 certificates or with Windows security. This subsystem is only used internally by the Service Fabric and is not directly accessible.

- **Testability subsystem**: The testability subsystem helps application developers test their services through simulated faults before and after deploying applications and services to production environments.

Is that all? There is a clear answer: no, because Service Fabric services are delivered and activated as a process by default, but they can also be offered as containers. So, you have the option to combine Azure microservices and Azure Container Services in your solution approaches. If you choose this option, the Azure Service Fabric works as an Orchestrator for Azure Container Services.

Microsoft itself uses this approach, for example, for its new Azure IoT Edge product.

 If you want more information about this and a complete reference implementation, then I recommend the following open source project: `https://github.com/dotnet-architecture/eShopOnContainers`.

Summary

In this chapter, we were introduced to the basic architectures behind the compute offers from the Azure platform (Azure VMs, Azure Container Services, Azure App Services, and Azure Service Fabric). We have also learned that services never act alone, but rather in the interaction of various Azure resources.

In the next chapter, we will learn all about Azure data services (basic knowledge, architecture, and use cases).

3
Data Storing and Processing

In the first chapter, I tried to give you an initial insight into the Azure platform with a comprehensive introduction. In the second chapter, we then followed with the question: Which technologies should we use?

The answers to this question fall into the following two areas:

- **Compute**: Compute is the area in which you deploy (host) your applications. This can, for example, be done as an Azure VM, but it is also conceivable within a microservices architecture.
- **Data storing and processing**: This area is easily explained. No application can exist today without being able to store and, if necessary, process data. This can, for example, be done by Azure Storage, but also by a more complex solution such as Azure Data Lake.

In the last chapter, we dealt with solutions in the area of compute. In this chapter, we will look at solutions in the area of data storing and processing.

In the computing area, the decision is made quickly—you know which solution you want to realize, briefly which approach (individual approach or combination) fits this solution and can start immediately.

In the data storing and processing area, the decision is much more complex. The reasons are very diverse and therefore, before I describe what Azure data services have to offer, I will first provide an introduction to the subject.

We will explore the following topics in detail in this chapter:

- Choosing the right data solution
- Which Azure data services are available?

 Offers available in the area of backup, site recovery, and so on, are not covered in this chapter.

Choosing the right data solution

Our first task is choosing the right data solution. Now the question immediately arises of: how do we approach this task?

Let's start with one of the big Vs. In our case, **V** is for **variety**.

What is variety?

The term **variety** describes the type and the nature of the data. For us, the following three types of data are relevant:

- **Structured data**: Structured data is defined in a data model or in any form of schema (schema-on-write model), where the data is described. As a solution for the structured data area, the Azure platform offers the so-called **Azure SQL as a service,** services.

- **Semi-structured data:** Semi-structured data does not have the formal structure of a data model, but contains tags or other types of markers to separate elements, and enforce hierarchies of records and fields within the data. Therefore, it is also known as the **self-describing structure**. Typical examples of a self-describing structure are XML or JSON. As a solution for the semi-structured data area, the Azure platform offers the so-called **Azure NoSQL as a service,** services, but the Azure SQL as a service offers are also able to handle this type of data.

- **Unstructured data:** Unstructured data refers to information that either does not have a pre-defined data model or is not organized in a pre-defined manner. Unstructured data is typically text heavy but may contain data such as dates, numbers, and facts as well. For example, unstructured data may include documents, metadata, health records, audio, video, analog data, images, files, and unstructured text (for example the body of an email message), or web pages. As a solution for the unstructured data area, the Azure platform uses the Azure Storage services, or in individual cases, Azure NoSQL as a service.

To meet our original objective, this means you must answer the following questions:

- What type of data are you intending to store? For example, common data types are transactional data, JSON objects, telemetry data, or flat files.
- Does your scenario have one or more data types that you need to store? An IoT scenario includes, for example, telemetry data, diagnostics and debugging data, device management data, and much more.

Where do we go from here? Let's look at another V of the big Vs. This time **V** is for **volume**.

What is volume?

The term **volume** describes the quantity of generated and stored data. The size of the data determines the value of a dataset and whether or not a dataset can be considered as big data.

To meet our original objective, this means you must answer the following questions:

- How large is the data you need to store?
- Entities should be maintained as a single document or multiple documents?

Where do we go next? We will leave the list of big Vs and deal now with a few rather specific factors. I will start with the factors, concurrency and consistency.

Concurrency and consistency

Let's start with the term **concurrency**. Here, you have to answer the following question: What kind of concurrency mechanism do you want to use?

The following options are available:

- **Pessimistic concurrency control**: In the case of pessimistic concurrency control, the application performs many updates, which can contain a high conflict potential. The mechanism you choose will try to counteract this with record locking.
- **Optimistic concurrency control**: In the case of optimistic concurrency control, there is no high conflict potential. Therefore, this mechanism provides only a simple timestamp lock.

The next term is **consistency** or rather, **consistency model**.

Consistency models are used in distributed systems or distributed data stores (such as a filesystem or a database). The consistency model specifies a contract between user and system, wherein the system guarantees that if the user follows the contract, the memory will be consistent and the results of memory operations will be predictable.

 I will address the topic of the consistency model later in this chapter, in the description of the Azure Cosmos DB.

Replication and redundancy

In order to guarantee stability and high availability, the customer's data in the Azure data center is replicated constantly. Before I introduce you to the mechanisms that Azure offers, first let's look at some theory:

- **Replication** refers to the multiple storage of the same data at mostly several different sites and the synchronization of these data sources.
- **Redundancy** is the additional presence of functionally identical or comparable resources of a technical system, which are not required where normal operation is trouble-free. In other words, redundancy is a direct result of successful replication.

We now come to the mechanisms already mentioned. The Azure platform offers you:

- **Locally redundant storage (LRS)**: LRS means that the data is held three times in one data center from one region. The LRS manages three copies of the customer's data to protect it from hardware failures. LRS does not protect the workloads from the failure of a whole data center.
- **Zone-redundant storage (ZRS)**: ZRS stores three copies of the customer's data as well as the LRS. The difference is that the data is guarded in two to three facilities. These facilities can be located in the same or in a different region. This concept provides more enhanced durability than LRS. The user profits from durability within a region.
- **Geo-redundant storage (GRS)**: An even higher durability can be achieved with GRS. GRS manages six copies of the user's data. The first three copies are replicated in the primary region. Additionally, another three copies are maintained in a secondary region which is located remotely from the primary region. This concept provides an even higher level of durability. This means that Azure failovers to the secondary region if a failure in the primary region should occur.
- **Read-access geo-redundant storage (RA-GRS)**: The replication to a secondary geographic location is provided with read access. The customer holds read access to the data, maintained in the secondary location. Access from the primary and the secondary region is possible. The RA-GRS is the default option for your storage account on creation.

The mechanisms just described are only valid for Azure Storage services. With the Azure SQL as a service offers, modified options come into action:

- Azure SQL Database, Azure SQL Elastic Database or Azure SQL Data Warehouse first use the Azure Backup service to create a full, differential, or transaction log backup
- Then, in a second step, the backup is stored in a storage account and saved with the mechanisms already described

The backups have a so-called **retention time**. Depending on the selected performance level, the availability ends after 7 days (standard level) or 35 days (premium level).

Azure PostgreSQL as a service and Azure MySQL as a service (both currently in the preview state) do not have the option of automatic backup. Here, you have to create a manual backup first and then you can save the backup files in the Azure Storage.

Other factors

You now know the most important criteria for selecting a data solution. However, there are many other questions whose answers can be used to make a decision.

To give you an idea, I have some examples:

Example 1—data relationships:

Typical questions in this area are as follows:

- Will your data need to support one-to-many or many-to-many relationships?
- Are relationships themselves an important part of the data?
- Will you need to join or otherwise combine data from within the same dataset, or from external datasets?

Example 2—availability:

Typical questions in this area are as follows:

- Does your solution need to be hosted in certain Azure regions?
- Is the service available in all Azure regions?

Example 3—hybrid scenarios and portability:

Typical questions in this area are:

- Is there a need to migrate data from or to on-premises, external data centers, or other cloud-hosting environments?

Which Azure data services are available?

In the first section, I gave you the necessary theoretical knowledge. Now, in the second part, we will look at the actual offer.

Let's take a look at the first diagram. Since the offer is very extensive, I have divided the area into nine categories:

- Management
- Processing
- Storage

- SQL as a service
- NoSQL as a service
- Big data
- Analytics
- **Artificial Intelligence (AI)**
- Virtualization

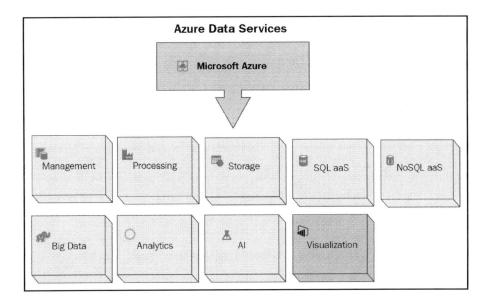

Management

The first category we will consider is **management** or **data management**. In general, the capabilities in the area of management are usually linked to the individual Azure data services themselves.

In some other cases, the management area is also linked to on-premises tools (for example, Azure SQL Database with the SQL Server Management Studio)

Now the question arises—what does this category do or why does the category exist at all?

Simple answer—there is still a special, cross-service offer, which I will introduce to you now, called **Azure Data Catalog**:

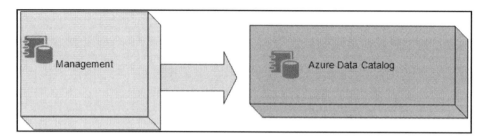

Azure Data Catalog

Azure Data Catalog is a fully managed service (for enterprises) whose users can discover the data sources they need and understand the data sources they find.

With Azure Data Catalog, any user (for example, business analyst, data scientist, or developer) can discover, understand, and consume data sources.

With Azure Data Catalog, you can register all your data sources and can contribute metadata and annotations to these entries. You can also define the relationships between the different data sources and control the access via a fine-grained legal system.

Processing

The next category we will consider is **processing** or **data processing**. What is it about? The term **data processing** refers to the process of gathering, organizing and transforming data for the purpose of extracting information or, generally, of information retrieval.

You can see the category of data processing is of central importance to our daily work.

The Azure platform currently has the following three offers in the portfolio:

- **Azure Data Factory**
- **Azure Stream Analytics**
- **Azure Time Series Insights**

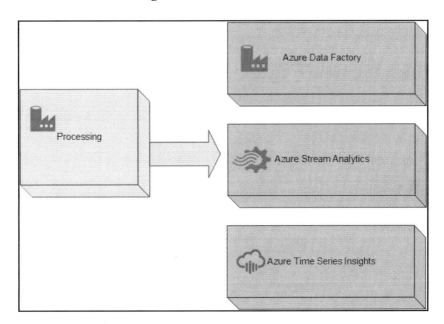

Azure Data Factory

Working with data is a complex issue and, therefore, it is not very easy to describe the Azure Data Factory service.

Let's start with a simple definition:

In general, a data factory allows you to process local data at the same time (for example from a SQL Server) along with data from the cloud (for example, from an Azure SQL Database, Blobs, and Tables). It does not matter whether the data is in a structured, semi-structured or unstructured form. The data sources (input datasets) are created, processed and monitored within the data factory via a simple, highly available data pipeline.

This is the simple definition, let's now come to a more complex definition:

Azure Data Factory is a cloud-based data integration service that lets you create data-driven workflows (so-called **pipelines**) in the cloud to orchestrate and automate data shifts and data transformations.

In more detail—with Azure Data Factory, you can create and plan data-driven workflows, collect data from different data stores (local and cloud data stores), process and transform data using services such as Azure HDInsight Hadoop, Spark, Azure Data Lake Analytics, and Azure Machine Learning, and provide the output data for data storage to data stores such as an Azure SQL Data Warehouse, so that it can be used by **business intelligence (BI)** applications like Microsoft PowerBI.

Let's look at the individual components of a data factory.

A data factory consists of:

- **Input datasets**: The so-called input datasets are the incoming data from the following data sources:
    - Azure Blob Storage
    - Azure CosmosDB
    - Azure Data Lake Store
    - Azure SQL Database
    - Azure SQL Data Warehouse
    - Azure Table Storage
    - Amazon Redshift
    - DB2
    - MySQL
    - Oracle
    - PostgreSQL
    - SAP Business Warehouse
    - SAP HANA
    - SQL Server
    - Sybase

- Teradata
- Cassandra
- MongoDB
- Amazon S3
- FTP
- **Hadoop distributed file system (HDFS)**
- **SSH File Transfer Protocol (SFTP)**
- Generic HTTP
- Generic OData
- Generic ODBC
- Salesforce
- Web table (HTML table)
- GE Historian

- **Linked services**: Before you can use your dataset, you must first create a linked service to link your data store to the data factory. Linked services define the connection information that is required by the data factory to connect to the external data store.
- **Pipeline**: A data factory has one or more pipelines. A pipeline is a logical group of activities that together form a task.
- **Activities**: Each pipeline has one or more activities. Activities define the actions that apply to your data. Currently, two types of activities are supported, which are as follows:
    - **Data movement activities**: This activity type is easily explained because it is limited to a pure copy operation between one of the available data sources and one of the available data sinks (both listed in the description of input datasets or output datasets)
    - **Data transformation activities**: The term data transformation activities describe the processes with which you can transform your raw data into predictions and insights and process them

Data transformation activities usually do not use their own codebase, but execute scripts (code) from the following services:

- Azure HDInsight Hive
- Azure HDInsight Pig
- Azure HDInsight MapReduce
- Azure HDInsight Streaming
- Azure HDInsight Spark.
- Azure Machine Learning (in combination with the Azure Batch Activity)
- Azure Data Lake Analytics (U-SQL Script)

Data transformation activities can also execute their own code, these are the activities based on:

- Stored procedure
- Custom .NET code

- **Output datasets**: The so-called **output datasets** are the outgoing data to one or more from the following data stores (data sinks):
  - Azure Blob Storage
  - Azure CosmosDB
  - Azure Data Lake Store
  - Azure SQL Database
  - Azure SQL Data Warehouse
  - Azure Table Storage
  - Oracle
  - SQL Server
  - File System

Because many data sources are located on the on-premises website, and therefore hybrid scenarios are the default case, Microsoft has introduced the Azure Data Factory Integration Runtime (formerly known as **Data Management Gateway**) as part of the Azure data services offering. You can download the free download here: `https://www.microsoft.com/en-us/download/details.aspx?id=39717a03ffa40-ca8b-4f73-0358-c191d75a7468=True751be11f-ede8-5a0c-058c-2ee190a24fa6=True`.

Azure Stream Analytics

The Azure Data Factory service provides a general tool for data processing on the Azure platform. However, the second offer which I will introduce to you now, is something more special.

What is Azure Stream Analytics?

Azure Stream Analytics is a real-time data processing tool for streaming data. This means in the cleartext: Azure Stream Analytics takes the data streams, analyzes them in its engine and makes them available to various receivers.

The data streams can come from devices, sensors, websites, social media feeds, applications, and much more. However, it is important to know that the data streams are never tapped directly; the access is always via an Azure IoT Hub and/or an Azure Event Hub.

Let's go to the processing of the data in the engine. This area is script-based and Azure Stream Analytics provides the Stream Analytics query language for this purpose. With the Stream Analytics query language, you can filter and sort the data, aggregate values, perform calculations, join data (within a stream or to reference data), and also use geospatial functions.

Not enough?

You can extend the capabilities by defining and calling additional functions. For example, you can define function calls for the Azure Machine Learning service to take advantage of your Azure Machine Learning solutions. You can also integrate **JavaScript user-defined functions** (**UDFs**) to make complex calculations as part of your processing.

In the context of processing, you also have the ability to add historical data or reference data to your process.

The last point refers to the availability of results for different recipients (consumers). In general, the output is always available for several receivers at the same time. So, you can in a single pass, pass data to a data store (for example, Azure Data Lake Store) to provide long-term archiving and simultaneously edit the data in Microsoft PowerBI.

Azure Time Series Insights

Let's go to the next tool in the Azure portfolio, the Azure Time Series Insights service. Azure Time Series Insight is also a real-time data processing tool (especially for IoT scenarios) and similar in design and functionality to the Azure Stream Analytics service.

The data can come from devices, sensors, applications, and more. It is important to know that the data is not collected directly; access is via an Azure IoT Hub and/or an Azure Event Hub. However, Azure Time Series Insight places great value on storing incoming data and then using it as historical data in the analysis process.

Storage

The next category in our introductory session is **storage**, on the Azure platform represented by the Azure Storage services. Azure Storage services are the oldest available data services (since the first preview of Azure 2008) and consist of the following individual offers:

- Azure Storage Blob service
- Azure Storage Blob service premium
- Azure Storage Queue service
- Azure Storage Table service
- Azure Files

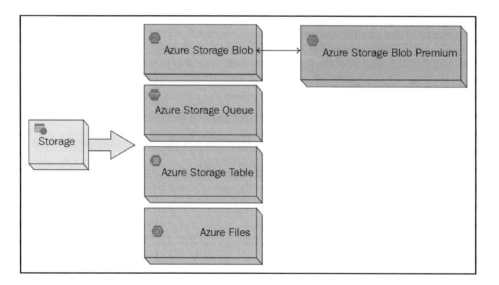

Azure Storage Blob service

The Azure Storage Blob service is for customers needing to store large sets of unstructured data. Because unstructured data is generally difficult to handle, the Azure Storage Blob service provides you with containers, an instrument for organizing the data.

Some facts about containers:

- The Azure Storage Blob service can use an indefinite count of containers.
- Each blob is assigned to one container.
- A container may contain an indefinite number of blobs. The only restriction is the capacity limit of the storage account.

Let's return to the subject of blobs. Three types of blobs are currently available:

- Block blobs
- Append blobs
- Page blobs

Block blobs are utilized for streaming and storing objects. They are best used for storing documents, media files, backups, and so on. Whereas block blobs are used for streaming and storing, append blobs fulfill the same task with the addition that they are optimized for append operations. Updating an append blob can only be done by adding a new block to the end. Append blobs' field of application consists of logging, in which data has to be written to the end of the blob. The third type of blob is the page blob. In most cases, page blobs are used to store VHD files for Azure IaaS VM solutions.

What else should I know about the Azure Storage Blob services?

When creating a blob storage account, you must set the Access-Tier attribute. Three types of access levels can be defined based on the data access pattern:

- **Hot access tier**: This level means that objects are kept in the storage account on a regular basis
- **Cool access tier**: This level indicates that objects in the storage account are less regularly retrieved
- **Archive access tier**: This level indicates that objects in the storage account are rarely accessed but must be stored for a long period of time to meet business continuity and compliance requirements (for example, medical records)

It is possible to switch, at any time, between these levels when a change in the usage pattern of the data makes this necessary.

Azure Storage Blob service premium

When creating a Blob storage account, there is a performance property available. This property decides whether a standard or a premium storage account is created. For most workloads, standard accounts are more than suitable, but in some cases, more I/O intensive applications need very fast storage. For such cases, the premium storage account was introduced. Premium storage is fully backed by SSD tiers and provides high performance, low latency storage.

Premium storage can currently only be used to store VHD files for Azure IaaS VM solutions. The performance property can't be changed after storage account creation, but it's possible to migrate VMs from the standard to premium storage tier.

Azure Storage Queue service

Azure Queue enables messaging between different parts of applications. This is used in the development of highly scalable and flexible applications. Components of applications are often decoupled, to enable independent scalability for the single parts.

Queues are also used as an asynchronous method of communication between components that run on different locations (cloud, on-premises, desktop, mobile). It's also possible to build workflows and asynchronous tasks.

A storage account has no limit on the number of queues, as well as the number of messages these contain, but a single message can only be up to 64 KB in size.

Azure Storage Table service

The Azure Storage Table service can be described as a NoSQL database. This means that the database has no schema and each value in a table has a typed property name. This property name can be used for filtering, sorting, and as selection criteria. There are multiple entities in a table that each consist of a collection of values and their property names.

Common scenarios for table storage are databases or datasets for web applications, collections of metadata, or bigger collections, for example, for customer data or for addresses.

Azure Files

The Azure Files service offers you a network file share in the cloud, by using industry standards like **Server Message Block (SMB)** protocol and **Common Internet File System (CIFS)**. So, you get a comparable offer otherwise provided by conventional Windows or Samba file servers.

An Azure File share can be used from multiple computers and by multiple users simultaneously. The difference is that the users don't have to be connected to the company network anymore. An Azure File share can also be mounted concurrently by Azure VMs and on-premises deployments running Windows, macOS, or Linux. Common scenarios for Azure File shares are diagnostics or debugging data, shared application files, or simply temporary storage.

SQL as a service

The next category we will consider is SQL as a service. What is it about? Simple answer—all offers in this area are cloud-based versions of classic relational database systems. I would use the word classic, however, with reservation, since these systems today can also use data based on JSON, Geospatial, and similar.

The Azure platform currently has the following three offers in the portfolio:

- **Azure SQL Database**
- **Azure PostgreSQL**
- **Azure MySQL**

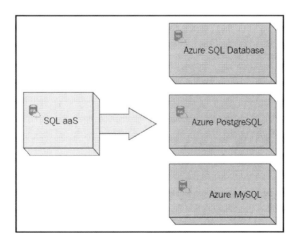

Azure SQL Database

Azure SQL Database is a fully managed cloud version of the Microsoft SQL Server engine.

But wait! Because Microsoft is driving a *cloud-first* strategy, the development of the Azure SQL Database is at all times ahead of the development of the Microsoft SQL Server. Only when a feature has established itself in the cloud, is it also adopted on the on-premises site.

What do I need to know? Regardless of the operation of the actual SQL Database server, each database is provided individually and isolated from the others, and has its own service level with a guaranteed performance level. The service level, and thus also the performance level, can be changed at any time.

Let's return to the terms **service level** and **performance level**—both are selection criteria, in the creation process of an Azure SQL Database. However, a service level is only a collection of performance levels, so we should be more concerned with the concept behind the term **performance level**.

How is a performance level defined? A performance level is defined by the number of permitted **Database Transaction Units** (**DTUs**). The second criterion formerly used, the so-called **transaction rate** (a metric from the **Azure SQL Database Benchmark** (**ASDB**) to capture the maximum transaction throughput per hour, minute, or second) will no longer be used.

What is a DTU? A definition of a DTU is a bit difficult, as it can be described as an object, but it is not actually a real object. DTUs are power units to which a certain percentage of the total performance of the database server is allocated in CPU, memory, and read or write rates.

The offered performance levels contain between 5 DTUs (at the basic service level) and 4,000 DTUs (in the premium service level P15). The larger the number of DTUs, the greater the performance of the database.

Another criterion for the selection of a performance level is the maximum size of the database. Also, the maximum size, which can reach the database, depends on the selected performance level.

The maximum size of the database per level is:

- **Basic**: 2 GB
- **Standard (S0 - S12)**: 250 GB
- **Premium (P1 - P6)**: 500 GB
- **Premium (P11 + P15)**: 4 TB
- **Premium RS**: 500 GB

Is that all now? No, also the number of simultaneously concurrent requests (maximum concurrent workers), the number of concurrent logins (maximum concurrent logins), and the number of concurrent sessions (maximum sessions) are limited per level.

- Since the Microsoft Ignite 2017 Conference (September 2017), the Azure SQL Database can also be used as a NoSQL (Graph) Database.
- At the Microsoft Ignite 2017 Conference (September 2017), the SQL R Services (part of the Azure SQL Database functionality) was renamed Machine Learning Service.
- Attention! This service is not identical to the previous Azure Machine Learning offer but part of a major restructuring of the offer.

SQL Server Stretch Database

The SQL Server Stretch Database is a special variant of the SQL Database for hybrid scenarios and comes into action when you need to store large amounts of transaction data from an on-premises SQL Server Database (starting with SQL Server 2016) over a long period of time (so-called **cold storage**) in the cloud.

As soon as you have activated the stretch functionality in your SQL Server, the data released for archiving will automatically be transferred to an Azure SQL Database.

For more information, visit `https://docs.microsoft.com/en-us/sql/sql-server/stretch-database/stretch-database`.

Azure PostgreSQL

Azure PostgreSQL as a service (currently in the preview state) is a fully managed cloud version of the popular open source database, PostgreSQL. Azure PostgreSQL as a service supports all open source management and deployment tools available in the community and is designed primarily for the development of highly scalable web applications.

Azure MySQL

Azure MySQL as a service (currently in the preview state) is a fully managed cloud version of the popular open source database MySQL. Azure MySQL as a service supports all open source management and deployment tools available in the community and is designed primarily for the development of highly scalable web applications (the most popular example is the blog engine, WordPress).

Other offers

I would like to introduce you to another two offerings. Both are based, just like the Azure SQL Database, on the Microsoft SQL Server Engine:

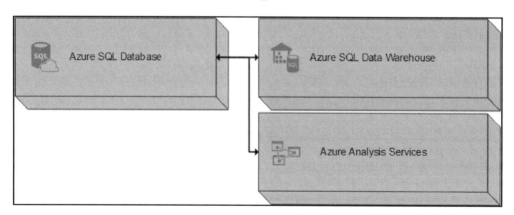

Azure SQL Data Warehouse: Azure SQL Data Warehouse is the cloud-based version of the SQL Server Data Warehouse and uses the same **Massively Parallel Processing (MPP)** architecture as the on-premises version.

For processing within the MPP architecture, SQL Data Warehouse distributes your data in the background to many shared-nothing storage and processing units.

Azure Analysis Services: Azure Analysis Services is the cloud-based version of the SQL Server Analysis Services. There are, however, two differences which are as follows:

- You can scale up the processing workflow in the cloud as needed
- You can extend the processing workflow, for example, with your Azure Machine Learning solutions

NoSQL as a service

The next category we will consider is NoSQL as a service. What is it about? Simple answer—the offers in this area are cloud-based versions of a NoSQL database system. A NoSQL database is primarily used to store semi-structured data.

The Azure Platform currently has the following offer in the portfolio, **Azure CosmosDB**:

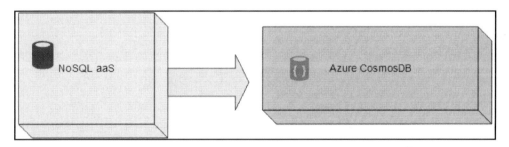

Azure CosmosDB

The Azure CosmosDB is a special case because it is not only a (prefabricated) service offer but also a toolkit with which you can create a service according to your individual needs. Let's have a look at the modular system in detail:

Azure CosmosDB is based on the **atom–record–sequence** (**ARS**) data model and is supported by multiple data models.

These include models for:

- **Key/value stores**: Key/value store is a large table which has a unique key to each data value and its uses this key to store the data by using appropriate hashing function. Most key/value stores only support query, insert, and delete operations. To update a value (partially or completely), a client must overwrite the existing data.
- **Document databases**: Document database and key/value store are almost similar except that there is a collection of named fields and data called as documents each of which could be simple or compound elements. Encoding of the data in fields are done using XML, YAML, JSON, BSON, or even stored as plain text. Enabling an application to query and filter data is possible using the fields since they are exposed to storage management system. The freeform approach that the document database provides makes it more flexible since the applications store different data in documents as the business requirements changes
- **Graph databases**: Nodes and edges are two types of information that graph database stores. Nodes can be considered as entities and edges specifies relationships between them. Both nodes and edges can have properties that provide information about that node or edge, similar to columns in a table. Edges can also have a direction indicating the nature of the relationship.

Furthermore, Azure CosmosDB provides support for numerous APIs:

- DocumentDB API
- MongoDB API
- Table API (Azure Storage Table service)
- Graph API (Apache TinkerPop Gremlin)
- Graph API (Apache Spark GraphX)

Further data models and APIs are planned.

Let's go back to the topic of **consistency**, or rather the consistency model. Distributed database systems typically provide the following two models:

- **Strong consistency**: Strong consistency provides guaranteed linearization, which means that the readings will definitely return the latest version of an element. In other words, a client can never see an unauthorized or incomplete write operation to ensure that he always accesses the most recent elements.

An Azure CosmosDB account that is configured to use strong consistency cannot associate with more than one Azure region.

- **Eventual consistency:** Eventual consistency ensures that the replication within the group ultimately leads to convergence in the absence of further writes. The eventual consistency level represents the weakest form of consistency, where a client may retrieve older values than those previously displayed. The eventual consistency layer provides the weakest read consistency, but the lowest latency for read and write operations.

An Azure CosmosDB account configured with eventual consistency can be assigned to any number of Azure regions.

Azure CosmosDB also provides the following models:

- **Bounded staleness**: The consistency level, bounded staleness, ensures that read operations that are against writing operations are less than a factor of K for the number of versions, or the factor T as a time interval. Bounded staleness is particularly recommended for globally distributed applications, with scenarios that require high consistency, but also 99.99% availability and low latency.

An Azure CosmosDB account configured with bounded staleness can be assigned to any number of Azure regions.

- **Session**: Unlike the other consistency models, the consistency level, session is only scoped to a client session. The sessions level guarantees monotonic reads, monotonic writes, and read-your-own-writes (RYW) guarantees. This gives you a predictable consistency for your session, a maximum readability, and a read and write speed with a low latency.

An Azure CosmosDB account configured with session can be assigned to any number of Azure regions.

- **Consistent prefix**: The consistency level, consistent prefix, guarantees, in the absence of further writing operations, that the replicas within the group ultimately come to convergence. It is also ensured that no write operations are displayed outside the specified sequence during read operations. When writing is done in the order *A, B, C*, the client displays *A, A, B* or *A, B, C* and does not display an *A, C,* or *B, A, C* sequence.

An Azure CosmosDB account configured with the consistent prefix can be assigned to any number of Azure regions. Some notes for developers:

- A common usage scenario for Azure CosmosDB applications is to track changes to data, update materialized views, perform real-time analysis, archive data in cold storage, and trigger notifications based on specific events based on these changes.
- In order to make it easy for you as a developer, Microsoft offers you the **Change Feed Processor Library** as an SDK.
  For more information, visit `https://docs.microsoft.com/en-us/azure/cosmos-db/change-feed`.
  To download, visit `https://www.nuget.org/packages/Microsoft.Azure.DocumentDB.ChangeFeedProcessor/`.
- Since the Microsoft Ignite 2017 Conference (September 2017), there is a first preview for an integration of Azure CosmosDB with Azure Functions. You now have the option to create trigger functions to handle events.
  For more information, visit `https://docs.microsoft.com/en-us/azure/cosmos-db/serverless-computing-database`.

Big data

The next category we will consider is *big data*. What is it about? A typical big data solution is designed to handle the ingestion, processing, and analysis of data that is too large or complex for traditional database systems.

The Azure platform currently has the following offers in the portfolio:

- **Azure HDInsight**
- **Azure Data Lake Store**
- **Azure Data Lake Analytics**

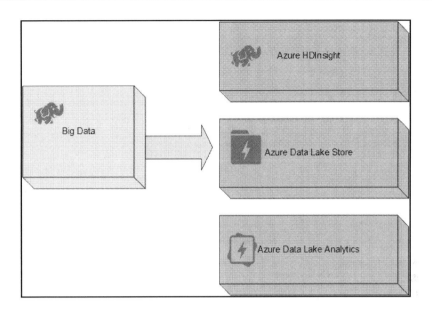

Azure HDInsight

Azure HDInsight is a complete cloud-based version of Apache Hadoop and is equivalent to the Hortonworks Data Platform Hadoop Distribution. Apache Hadoop is a framework for distributed processing and analysis of large datasets provided in clusters of computers.

Azure HDInsight currently supports the following cluster types:

- **Apache Hadoop**: Clusters based on Apache Hadoop use the HDFS, the YARN resource management, and the MapReduce programming model. A cluster based on Apache Hadoop is for parallel processing and analysis of batch data.
- **Apache Spark**: Apache Spark is a framework for parallel processing that supports in-memory processing to increase the performance of applications for analyzing large amounts of data. Spark works with SQL, data streams, and machine learning datasets.
- **Apache HBase**: Apache HBase is a Hadoop-based NoSQL database that provides random access and strong consistency for large amounts of unstructured and partially structured data, and that is in a potential dimension of billions of lines, multiplied by billions of columns.

- **Machine Learning Server (formerly known as Microsoft R Server)**: The Machine Learning Server is a server for hosting and managing parallel, distributed R processes. This feature allows data scientists, statisticians, and R programmers to access scalable, distributed analysis methods in HDInsight, as needed.
- **Apache Storm**: Apache Storm is a distributed real-time calculation system for the fast processing of large data streams and is offered as a managed cluster in HDInsight.
- **Apache Interactive Hive**: This is an in-memory cache for interactive and faster Hive queries.
- **Apache Kafka**: Apache Kafka is an open source platform for creating streaming data pipelines and applications, as well as providing a message queue function that allows you to publish and subscribe data streams.

Azure Data Lake Store

Azure Data Lake Store is a huge repository for enterprises and is used in all kinds of big data analysis workloads. Azure Data Lake Store provides you with the ability to capture data of any size, type, and acquisition speed, to perform operational and exploratory analyses in a single location.

Some more details—the Azure Data Lake Store is an Apache Hadoop file system that is compatible with HDFS and can be used with the complete Hadoop ecosystem. This means you can easily integrate your existing HDInsight applications or services into your Azure Data Lake Store.

Azure Data Lake Store can store any data in the system's native format without prior transformation. Azure Data Lake Store does not require defining a schema before loading the data. The interpretation of the data and definition of a schema is performed at the time of the analysis by the individual analysis frameworks (for example, MapReduce).

Azure Data Lake Store can manage structured, partially structured, and unstructured data, by storing files of any size, up to a **petabyte (PB)** size, and format.

Azure Data Lake Analytics

Azure Data Lake Analytics is a new analysis service for big data, with the focus of the service being on the logic of your applications (reaching your business goals) and not being affected by the complexity of the necessary infrastructure.

Similar to the Azure Data Lake Store, there is no limit to the size of individual records in the Azure Data Lake Analytics service.

Azure Data Lake Analytics is a build-on for Apache YARN (a subproject of Apache Hadoop) that allows the use of multiple data processing engines.

With Azure Data Lake Analytics, U-SQL (a combination of C# and SQL) is introduced as a new programming language for big data scenarios.

Azure Data Lake Analytics (and U-SQL) is fully integral in a Visual Studio edition of your choice with the Azure Data Lake Tools for Visual Studio.

Analytics

The next category we will consider is *analytics*. What is it about? Analytics, or rather, data analytics, is designed to explore large amounts of data of different types to discover hidden patterns, unknown correlations, and other useful information. Such information can help you reach your business goals and bring you competitive advantages over competitors, such as more effective marketing or higher sales.

The Azure platform currently has the following offers in the portfolio:

- **Cortana Intelligence Suite**
- **Azure Stream Analytics**
- **Azure Data Lake Analytics**
- **Azure Time Series Insights**

This category overlaps in its offers with the processing and big data categories. The reason for this is that Microsoft tries to offer services as a complete solution for a workload.

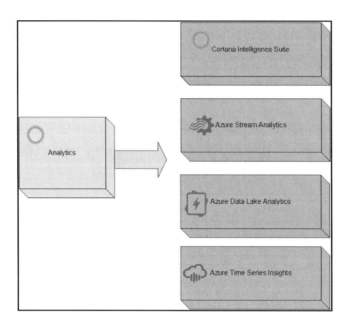

Cortana Intelligence Suite

First of all, the Cortana Intelligence Suite is not a new offer, but a special collection of all relevant Azure services (such as Azure Data Factory, Azure Machine Learning, and Azure Data Lake). With the suite, you get a complete set of tools for companies to help transform your data into intelligent actions (action requirements) by providing big data and advanced analytics functions.

The Cortana Intelligence Suite offers even more:

- With the Microsoft **Team Data Science Process** (**TDSP**) you get an agile, iterative, data science process for executing and delivering advanced analytics solutions
- The TDSP is a systematic method that describes a sequence of work steps (within the Cortana Intelligence Suite or the Azure platform) that are important for the development of predictive models or intelligent applications

- The individual work steps serve as a guide to defining the problem, analyzing relevant data, creating and evaluating prediction models, and then providing these models in intelligent applications

TDSP is iterative, which means the understanding of new or existing optimizations in the model generally develops continuously, and thus also requires the constant reworking of previously concluded work steps.

What else do you need to know? Your own existing processes, for example, project planning processes, can be easily integrated into the defined step sequence.

> You can find all sources of the Microsoft TDSP at `https://github.com/Azure/Microsoft-TDSP`.

Not enough? So that you can start right away with your work, the so-called Cortana Intelligence Suite Industry Solutions are included in the offer. These are templates for industry-specific advanced analytics solutions (for example, predictive maintenance) and can be used as a starting point for your own solutions.

> You can find all sources for the *Cortana Intelligence Suite Industry Solutions* here: `https://github.com/Azure/Cortana-Intelligence-Suite-Industry-Solution-How-To-Guides`.

As I have already provided the description of the products, Azure Stream Analytics, Azure Data Lake Analytics and Azure Time Series Insights, in other sections of this chapter, I won't cover them again here.

AI

The next category we will consider is *AI*. In general, AI is an attempt to replicate a human-like intelligence, that is, to create an application that is able to process problems on its own.

The Azure platform currently has the following three offers in the portfolio:

- **Azure Machine Learning**
- **Cognitive Services**
- **Bot Framework**

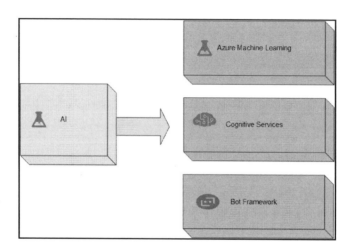

Azure Machine Learning

Azure Machine Learning (**Azure ML**) is a cloud service that helps you create predictive analytics solutions.

For those who do not have an economics degree, predictive analytics analyzes behavior patterns from the past, based on large amounts of data and creates predictions and forecasts for future events. In short, predictive analytics combines your data with mathematical models. The fields of application for predictive analytics are, for example, insurance, financial services, and commerce. The Azure ML service is, therefore, a tool for mathematicians and statisticians (also known as **data scientists**) in the analysis departments of companies.

What is included in the offer?

- The managed Azure ML service
- An integrated development environment (**ML Studio**)
- A collection of *Best of Breed* algorithms (developed by Microsoft research, the XBox Team and Bing) as built-in

- Support for custom R code
- Support for custom Python code
- Support for Azure ML templates

 What are Azure ML Templates? The question is not quite as easy to answer. Therefore, we should first ask ourselves: What is not an Azure ML Template? An Azure ML template is not an Azure ML Sample Experiment. Azure ML Sample Experiments usually provide an insight into individual aspects of Machine Learning, while an Azure ML Template is a reflection of industry best practices and consists of several individual steps (data treatment, data processing, technology, function, training, and deployment) respectively corresponding to Azure ML Experiments. Each Azure ML Template contains the following elements:

- A data schema for the specific domain
- A collection of preconfigured Azure ML modules
- A collection of Custom R scripts integrated into the Execute R Script Module

- Support for several hundred Open Source R Packages
- A collection of quick start samples

 All available quick starts, Azure ML templates, examples and various other material can be found here: `https://gallery.cortanaintelligence.com/`.

Cognitive Services

Cognitive Services (also known as **Project Oxford**) is a collection of technologies (delivered in the form of preconfigured solutions) that make the development of applications smarter.

The following services (APIs) are currently components of the collection (only a selection):

- Face APIs
- Computer vision APIs
- Speech APIs
- **Language Understanding Intelligent Service (LUIS)**
- Emotion APIs

- Spellcheck APIs
- Video APIs
- Speaker recognition APIs
- **Custom Recognition Intelligent Service (CRIS)**
- Web Language Model APIs
- Bing Autosuggest API
- Bing Spell Check API
- Bing Search APIs
- Bing Web Search API
- Bing Image Search API
- Bing Video Search API
- Bing News Search API

 You can find a complete list (with detailed information) here: `https://azure.microsoft.com/en-us/services/cognitive-services/`. You can find a list with currently available PoCs for new services here: `https://labs.cognitive.microsoft.com/`.

Bot Framework

The Bot Framework is an open source offering from Microsoft for building Bots (or Bot Applications), the word **Bots** comes from **robots**. With a Bot, you communicate with your users in a natural language, for example, through a website, through Skype for Business, and more.

 You can download the source code here: `https://github.com/Microsoft/BotBuilder`.

With the Azure Bot service, a cloud version of the Bot Framework is available.

Virtualization

The last category in our introduction is *virtualization*. Actually, the term is misleading because the category also includes *reporting* and *creating dashboards*.

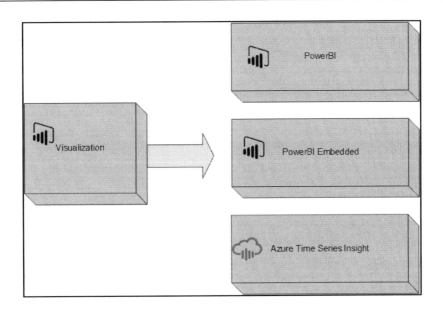

PowerBI

First of all, Microsoft PowerBI is not an Azure offer.

Microsoft PowerBI is part of the already rich SaaS offer from Microsoft, and to be precise, Microsoft Power BI is part of the Microsoft Business Platform (also known as **Microsoft Business Application Platform**).

Microsoft PowerBI is a suite of tools for analyzing and visualizing business data and sharing insights (reporting and dashboards) on various device types.

For this purpose, Microsoft Power BI offers the following so-called building blocks:

- Data Sources (Datasets)
- Reports
- Visualizations
- Dashboards
- Tiles

PowerBI Embedded

With the PowerBI Embedded offer (an Azure offer) you have the ability to integrate a PowerBI dashboard into an Azure application of your choice (for example, an Azure Web App).

Azure Time Series Insights

This is not really an independent offer as Azure Time Series Insights uses the capabilities of Microsoft PowerBI internally.

Summary

In this chapter, I've provided you with the basic information on data storing and processing. You've had an answer to the question: *Choose the right data solution?* And, in another section, you got an overview of *Which Azure data services are available.*

In the next chapter, you will learn all about Azure Virtual Networking (basic knowledge, architecture, and use cases).

4

Networking Design and Management

In the last three chapters, I have tried to give you a more in-depth look at the Azure platform with a comprehensive introduction. In this chapter, we will explore the question: How do I properly link the components of the Azure platform so, they work seamlessly together?

A simple answer: With the Azure **Virtual Network** (**VNet**) application building block, the Azure platform offers the right solution for this.

However, Azure VNet is more than just a simple service. Because of its complexity, you can realize all conceivable scenarios. Individual needs are not a hindrance, but only a matter of adjustment.

We will explore the following topics in detail in this chapter:

- Anatomy of a VNet infrastructure
- Connectivity
- Internet connectivity
- Connectivity between Azure resources
    - Azure VNet peering
    - Azure global VNet peering
    - Azure VNet-to-VNet (VPN gateway)

- On-premises connectivity
    - Azure Point-to-Site
    - Azure Site-to-Site
    - Azure ExpressRoute
- Azure VNet service endpoints
- Routing, load balancing, or more general traffic directions
    - User-defined routes
    - Routing using the **border gateway protocol (BGP)**
    - Azure Load Balancer
    - Azure Traffic Manager
    - Azure Application Gateway
- Security
    - **Network security groups (NSG)**
    - Application security groups
- Security infrastructure
    - **Network virtual appliance (NVA)**
- Management and monitoring
    - Microsoft **Operations Management Suite (OMS)**
    - Azure Monitor
    - Azure Network Watcher

Anatomy of a VNet infrastructure

Before starting with the detailed analysis of the topic, in this section of the chapter, I would like to introduce you to the typical anatomy of a VNet infrastructure. You will get to know the individual components of a VNet and their respective relationships to each other or to the public space. By acquiring this basic knowledge, you will then easily understand the subsequent sections of the chapter. Let's take a look at the following diagram:

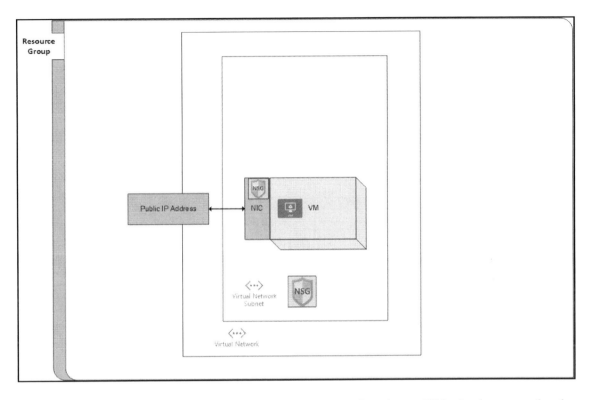

In the illustration, you can see a simple representation of an Azure VNet in the example of VNet support for Azure VMs.

Note that this example is generally valid, as the VNet support for most other Azure resources are also technologically based on the network capabilities of an Azure VM.

Azure resources currently supported by the Azure VNet:

- Azure Linux or Windows VMs
- Azure VM scale sets
- Azure Cloud Services
- Azure Service Fabric
- Azure Container Service
- Azure HDInsight
- Azure App Service (coming soon)
- Azure App Service environment
- Azure Redis Cache

- Azure API Management
- Azure Active Directory Domain Services
- Azure Batch
- Azure VPN gateway
- Azure Application Gateway (only internal)

The Azure Container Service, by default, creates its own VNet. However, you can create a custom VNet and use it with your created Azure Container Service.

Let's look at the details. The mandatory elements of an Azure VNet architecture are the following:

- **Resource group**: A resource group is a container that holds all related resources. For our example, this means that the resource group contains all elements of the virtual network and the application (the VM).

This is only a simplified illustration. It can be useful to distribute your solution across several resource groups.

A typical example of a solution distribution would be as follows:

- One resource group for the application
- One resource group for storage elements (optional)
- One resource group for the infrastructure (these are the VNet elements)
- One resource group for management elements (optional)

Best practice: Share your solution into at least one resource group for the VNet (and its individual components), and one resource group for the application (for example, Azure VM, Azure App Service App, and so on).

- **VNet**: An answer to the question, what is an Azure VNet? Is not so easy to find, because a VNet is not a service in the classical sense. Instead, a VNet is an individual collection of single components or services that are grouped together in a logical group (the VNet).

There is a second description, which we can consider as a fitting answer; a VNet is a representation of your own network in the cloud, or an extension of your on-premises network towards the cloud.

What do I need to know about VNets? A VNet is always run in isolation on the Azure platform. This allows you, on the one hand, to create multiple VNets using the same **Classless Inter-Domain Routing (CIDR)** address blocks (for example, to provide separate VNets for development, test, and production), or on the other hand, to create multiple VNets that access different CIDR address blocks, but which have the right to communicate with each other.

A VNet can be segmented into any number of VNet Subnets. When you create a VNet, you enter a custom IP address space that contains both public and private IP addresses. Azure allocates resources associated with the VNet to a private IP address from the address space that you assign.

Although communication can occur within a VNet or between multiple VNets over IP addresses, it is much easier to use names that are easy to remember and do not change. For the name resolution, the Azure platform uses an internal name service, or you have the ability to integrate your own DNS server. A VNet subnet is a logical unit (a segment) of the VNet, and is assigned with a part of the VNet address space.

 Best practice: You should equip your VNet with at least one subnet (as a host for the Azure resource).

- **Network Interface (NIC)**: The NIC enables the resources to communicate with the virtual network. One NIC is provided automatically when the resource is created. Other NICs can be added at any time to meet your needs.

  What do I need to know about NICs? You can link multiple public and/or private IPs with a NIC (dynamic or static). You can link a **Virtual IP (VIP)** for load balancing with a NIC (dynamic or static). You can get the MAC address of your NIC over the phase between stop and restart persistent.

Optional resources of an Azure VNet are the following:

- **Public IP address**: A public IP address is needed to communicate with the resource, for example, over the **Remote Desktop Service (RDP)**.
- NSG: An NSG is used to allow or deny network traffic. You can associate an NSG with an individual NIC or with a VNet subnet. If you associate it with a VNet subnet, the NSG rules apply to all VMs in that subnet. (More information on this topic will follow in a later section of the chapter.)

Now, you've learned everything about a VNet for a single VM, but in real life, there are usually more than just one. What does this mean for us and our example? If you thought that you simply have to provide the same Azure resources, the answer is only partially correct. There are differences and I will introduce those now. Take a look at the following diagram:

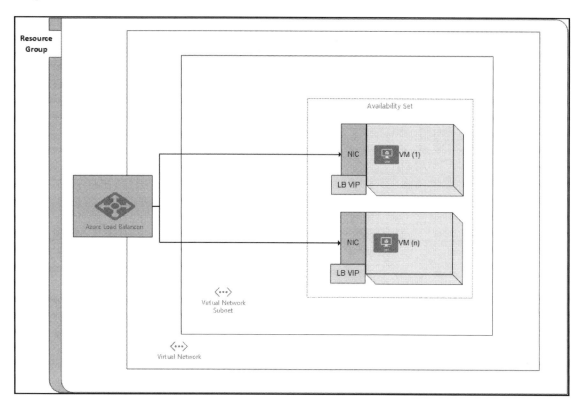

We start with the most important innovation in this illustration, which is Azure availability sets.

The availability sets are an organizational component (resource) of the Azure platform and manage the operation of two or more instances of a VM. The availability sets ensure that the VM instances are always running on different fault and update domains of the Azure platform, so that at least one instance is always online.

 Fault domain: A fault domain in Azure means that all servers in these domains run in the same fire sections, with the same air conditioning or electrical source. This means that all physical servers within in those domains can have an outage at the same time.
Update domain: An update domain in Azure means that all physical servers in an update domain will get updates such as firmware, drivers, and OS updates at the same time.

Let's look at the next novelty in this illustration: if you look closely, you can see an instance of the Azure Load Balancer serving as a new entry point to the architecture. The load balancer has the task of forwarding incoming internet requests to the provided VMs.

The load balancer requires the following additional resources to perform its tasks:

- **Public IP address**: A public IP address is needed for the load balancer to receive internet traffic.
- **Frontend configuration**: This associates the public IP address with the load balancer.
- **Backend address pool**: This contains a list of the NICs for all resources that will receive the incoming traffic. The assignment to the NICs usually takes place via so-called VIPs, but can also be defined via public or private IPs.

Not shown in the picture are the following resources:

- **Load balancer rules**: Load balancer rules are used to distribute network traffic among all the resources in the backend address pool.
- **Network address translation (NAT) rules**: NAT rules are used to route traffic to a specific resource. But beware if you want to enable, for example, the RDP for your VMs, you must create a separate NAT rule for each VM.

Now, we know all of the basics, it is time to make a complex architecture (N-tier architecture) out of this. Let's take a look at the following diagram:

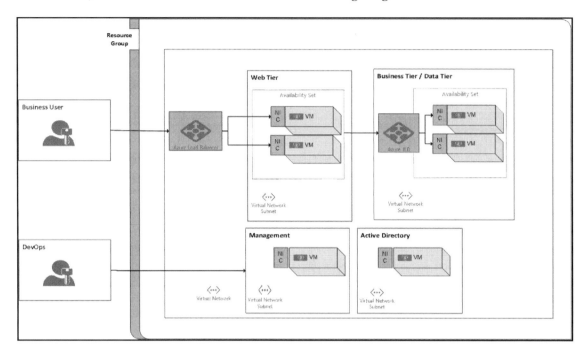

What is different here? The architecture is again based on the pattern for *multiple resources*, but this time, the design is repeated several times because the architecture is divided into, at least, the following three levels:

- Web Tier or frontend-application
- Business Tier or business logic
- Data Tier

The following levels are not required, but nevertheless often present:

- Management tier
- Active Directory

Actually, all existing levels within this architecture are also single subnets of the VNet.

The entry point for this architecture is, again, the Azure Load Balancer, which is only used to distribute incoming internet traffic to the web tier; the Azure **Internal Load Balancer** (**ILB**) is then used for all other levels.

 Unlike the Azure Load Balancer, the ILB requires a private IP address. To give the ILB a private IP address, create a frontend configuration and associate it with the subnet for the business tier.

Let's go back to *distribution from incoming internet traffic*. Not visible but still present, are the numerous NSGs that are respectively associated with the subnet. An NSG is used to regulate network traffic by allowing or denying network traffic. For our architecture, this means, for example, that you can use the help of an NSG to decide that the data from the web tier, can only be passed on to the business tier.

Now, I have some additional information about the optional architectural layers:

- **Management tier (also known as jumpbox or bastion host)**: The management tier includes a secure VM on the network that administrators (or DevOps) use to connect to the other VMs. Note that most of the time, the management tier has an NSG that allows remote traffic only from public IP addresses on a safe list. The NSG should also permit the use of the RDP. The management tier is also a good place to install a monitoring solution, such as Nagios or Zabbix, that can give you an insight into response time, VM uptime, and the overall health of your system.
- **Active Directory** tier: This includes a VM with an installed **Active Directory Domain Service** (**AD DS**). An Active Directory tier is only required if you use an SQL Server **AlwaysOn Availability Group** as a **Data Tier**. Prior to Windows Server 2016, SQL Server **AlwaysOn Availability Groups** must be joined to a domain. This is because availability groups depend on the **Windows Server Failover Cluster** (**WSFC**) technology.

 Windows Server 2016 provides the ability to create a failover cluster without Active Directory. If your architecture is based on Windows Server 2016, the AD DS server is not required.

In conclusion, I would like to present you with a variant of N-tier architecture: N-Tier architecture – multi-regions. This variant is designed for high availability and as a disaster recovery infrastructure. Let's take a look at the following diagram:

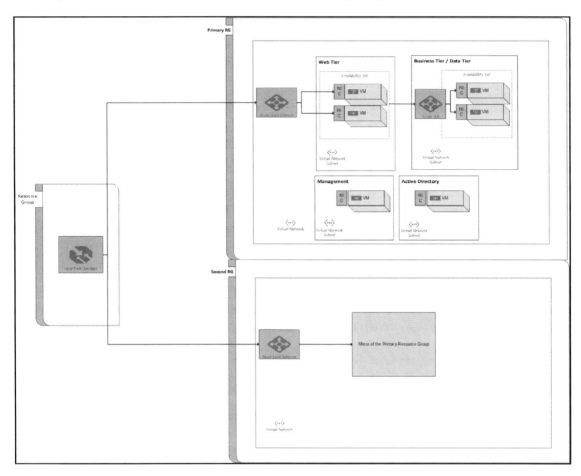

What is different here? The architecture shown here is divided into three resource groups. Two resource groups (located in two Azure regions) are based on the already presented N-tier architecture and are thus identical.

One of these resource groups is called **primary resource group** and is for daily use. The other resource group (called **secondary resource group**) serves as a failover.

The third resource group only includes an instance of Azure Traffic Manager as a resource. Azure Traffic Manager is the new entry point for this architecture and routes incoming requests to one of the regions. During normal operations, it routes requests to the primary resource group. If that region becomes unavailable, the traffic manager fails over to the secondary resource group.

Not shown in the figure but still mostly available, is the VPN gateway connection between the **Primary RG** and **Second RG**. With this VNet-to-VNet connection, you can enable network traffic between the two VNets, and a type of synchronization.

Where do we go from here? In the last section of the chapter, I tried to introduce you to the basic architectures from the area of Azure networking. You now know the individual components of a VNet (or at least most of them) and have thus acquired a certain basic knowledge of the topic.

In the next sections of the chapter, we will now discuss some aspects of the topic again, this time, in detail. We will begin with the area of *Connectivity*.

Connectivity

Connectivity is used to describe all processes for establishing communication channels, to or within the VNet. At present, we know three types of connectivity:

- Internet connectivity
- Connectivity between Azure resources (internal connectivity)
- On-premises connectivity

Internet connectivity

All Azure resources that are connected to a VNet, have an internet connectivity in the outgoing direction by default. The private IP address used by the resource is translated into a public IP address by the Azure infrastructure via a **Source Network Address Translation (SNAT)** operation.

In order to be able to communicate with Azure resources over the internet in the incoming direction, you must assign a public IP address for the resource to your VNet.

Connectivity between Azure resources (internal connectivity)

Internal connectivity is the main area in the connectivity sector, because, without communication between Azure resources, no solution would work and ultimately, there would be no Azure network.

At present, the internal connectivity area consists of the following offers:

- Azure VNet peering
- Azure global VNet peering
- Azure VNet-to-VNet (VPN gateway)

Azure VNet peering

Azure VNet peering is an option to connect different Azure VNets that work in the same Azure data center. Azure VNet peering lets you directly link two VNets in the same region via private IPs. Azure VNet peering routes packets between virtual networks through the internal Azure backbone network. An Azure VPN gateway between these networks is not needed.

This allows you a low-latency, high-bandwidth connection between virtual machines in the virtual networks. Azure VNet peering works with VNets based on the **Azure Resource Manager (ARM)** and/or the classical **Azure System Management (ASM)**.

Azure VNet peering also works across virtual networks in different subscriptions. So, you are able to connect, for example, subscriptions paid by different departments.

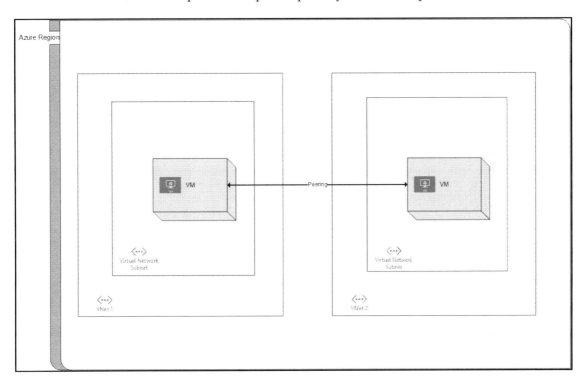

Azure global VNet peering

Azure global VNet peering is a variant of Azure VNet peering. While Azure VNet peering can only connect to the same region, you can also create connections between regions with Azure global VNet peering. In all other respects, Azure global VNet peering is the same.

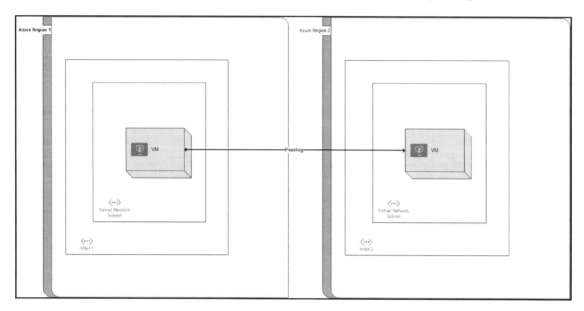

Azure VNet-to-VNet (VPN gateway)

The VNet-to-VNet (VPN gateway) connection is the oldest offer in the field of internal connectivity. A separate subnet with an installed VPN gateway is set up in each VNet you want to connect. An IPsec/IKE tunnel can then be provided as a secure line between these VPN gateways.

I have two pieces of important information:

- Data traffic via the VPN gateway is limited according to the selected service level
- The virtual networks may be in the same or different regions and may come from the same or different subscriptions

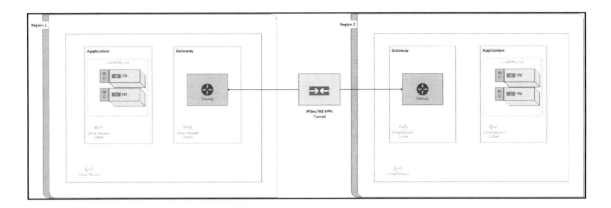

On-premises connectivity

On-premises connectivity is another main area in the connectivity sector, but only when it comes to the realization of hybrid scenarios. In everyday life, however, this is the usual situation.

At present, the on-premises connectivity area consists of the following offers:

- Azure Site-to-Site
- Azure Point-to-Site
- Azure ExpressRoute

Azure Site-to-Site

The Azure Site-to-Site VPN gateway connection is a similar connection type to Azure VNet-to-VNet, only that this time it is not a gateway subnet that is the goal of the connection setup, but it is a local VPN gateway that gets into your on-premises network.

In the Azure Site-to-Site connection, an IPsec/IKE tunnel is also provided as a secure line between the two gateways. For this connection to be established, the local VPN gateway must have a public IP.

A note of caution: Data traffic performance is unpredictable, as traffic flows over the internet.

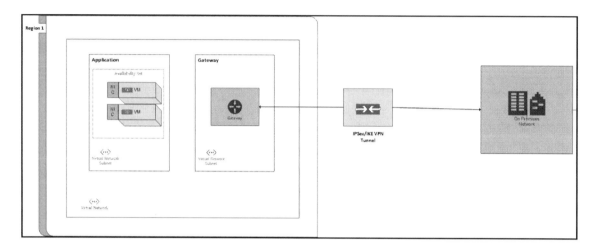

In the documentation for Azure networking, you can also find the term, Azure Site-to-Multi Site. This is a variant of the Azure Site-to-Site connection type and uses the VNet VPN gateway to simultaneously serve several local VPN devices.

The number of possible IPsec/IKE tunnels, and thus the connected elements, that can be attached to a VPN gateway is dependent on the selected service level maximum of 30 pieces.
If you are planning an Azure Site-to-Multi Site scenario, you must configure your VNet VPN gateway as **RouteBased**.

Azure Point-to-Site

Azure Point-to-Site is another version of Azure Site-to-Site, but has three important differences from the original which are as follows:

- This time, the destination of the connection setup is not a gateway subnet or a local VPN gateway. This time the destination of the connection setup is a VPN client installed on a single computer somewhere in your local network.

- Azure Point-to-Site does not use an IPSec/IKE tunnel for the secure connection between the two vertices, but a so-called **Point-to-Site (P2S)** SSTP tunnel. **Secure Socket Tunneling Protocol (SSTP)**, is an SSL-based protocol and has the advantage that it can penetrate firewalls, as most firewalls open the TCP port 443 used by SSL.
- Before Azure accepts a P2S connection, the user must first be authenticated. Azure offers two mechanisms for authentication:
    - Native Azure certificate authentication
    - Authentication using AD DS and a RADIUS server (Preview)

One update: Since the Microsoft Ignite 2017 Conference is also a preview for an IPSec/IKE v.2 (version 2.0) tunnel available, this preview also allows a P2S connection to a VPN client on a computer with a macOS operating system.

Note that the number of possible P2S SSTP tunnels (and thus, the connected elements), that can be attached to a VPN gateway is dependent on the selected service level of a maximum of 128 pieces.

Caution: Data traffic performance is unpredictable, as traffic flows over the internet.

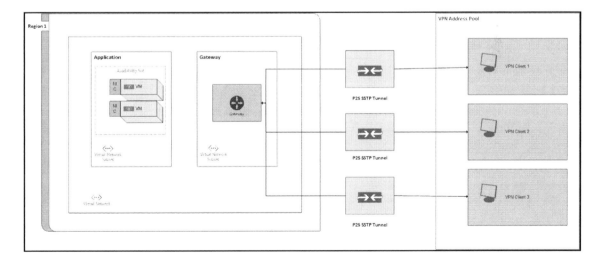

Azure ExpressRoute

Let's go to the last option of on-premises connectivity: Azure ExpressRoute. To make it clear: Azure ExpressRoute is in no way comparable to the Azure Site-to-Site or Azure Point-to-Site connections. So, the question arises: What is Azure ExpressRoute? Azure ExpressRoute is a service that allows you to establish a private connection between a Microsoft Data Center and the infrastructure on site or in a collocation environment.

Azure ExpressRoute connections do not take place over the public internet. This provides you with a greater security, a greater reliability, and a faster speed with less latency than a traditional internet connection.

Let's look at Azure ExpressRoute once in detail. The following diagram shows an example of a typical Azure ExpressRoute environment:

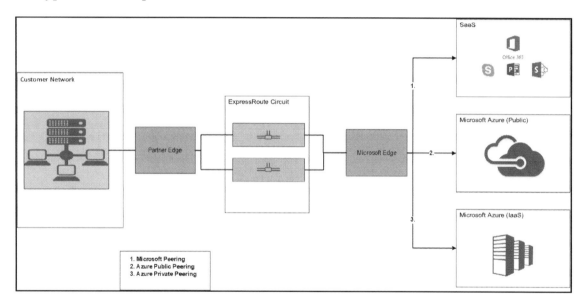

What can you see in the diagram? The starting point of our architecture is your **Customer Network** (or on-premises network), which is connected to a **Partner Edge**. The **Partner Edge** is an **Internet service provider** (**ISP**) solution and offers you technologies called **Multi-Protocol Label Switching** (**MPLS**) or ISP IP VPN.

MPLS is a type of data-carrying technique for telecommunications networks that directs data from one network to the next, based on short path labels rather than long network addresses. This technology avoids long and complex routing tables. The labels identify virtual links between distant nodes. MPLS can encapsulate packets of various network protocols; that's why it is named multi-protocol. MPLS supports nearly all common access technologies, including T1/E1, ATM, frame relay, and dark fiber connects, into points of presence or DSL.

The partner edge is then connected to Microsoft Edge via the so-called **ExpressRoute Circuit**, that represents a logical connection between your on-premises infrastructure and Microsoft cloud services through a connectivity provider. The Azure ExpressRoute circuit is rented by you for a certain range. What many do not know is that from Microsoft you get this bandwidth but delivered twice as an active/active connection to your internet service provider.

An Azure ExpressRoute circuit (or Azure ExpressRoute connection) has multiple routing domains (or peering types): a public Azure routing domain, a private Azure routing domain, and Microsoft routing domains.

All routing domains are configured identically for high availability on a router pair (with an active/active configuration or a payload distribution configuration).

Now I have some more details on the theme of peering. The three peering types are:

- **Microsoft peering**: Microsoft peering includes the connectivity to all Microsoft SaaS offers (such as Office 365 or Dynamics CRM). You can enable bidirectional connectivity between your WAN and Microsoft Cloud Services through the Microsoft peering routing domain.
- **Azure public peering**: Azure public peering includes all Azure PaaS offers such as Azure Storage, Azure SQL Databases, and Azure Web Apps that provide a public IP address. You can privately connect to services hosted on public IP addresses, including VIPs of your cloud services, through the public peering routing domain. You can connect the public peering domain to your **demilitarized zone (DMZ)** and connect to all Azure services on their public IP addresses from your WAN without having to connect through the internet.
- **Azure private peering**: Azure compute services, namely virtual machines and cloud services that are deployed within a virtual network, can be connected through the private peering domain. The private peering domain is considered to be a trusted extension of your core network into Microsoft Azure. You can set up bidirectional connectivity between your network and Azure virtual networks.

At the moment, Microsoft is trying to merge the peering types, Azure public peering and Microsoft peering (Preview).

Azure VNet service endpoints

The VNet service endpoints feature offers you the ability to integrate PaaS services without public IP directly into your VNet. A private address is assigned to the service endpoint and this IP is directly linked to your VNet. The connection via the internet is thus no longer possible for this PaaS service.

However, for the connection, the PaaS service and the VNet must be located in the same Azure region. Inter-regional endpoints are not possible. The feature is currently still in the preview status and only works with the services, Azure Storage and Azure SQL Database (or Azure SQL Data Warehouse), but further services are already in the pipeline.

Important note

In the last section of the chapter, I introduced you to all available connectivity options. Each of these options, I presented to you individually to make you more familiar with the details. However, I must now point out to you, none of these options is used individually in a real scenario.

Instead, a real-life scenario (a complex workload) is always an arbitrary combination of these options. Take a look at the following diagram, which shows a typical linking of the cloud with your **Headquarters** and your **Branch Office**:

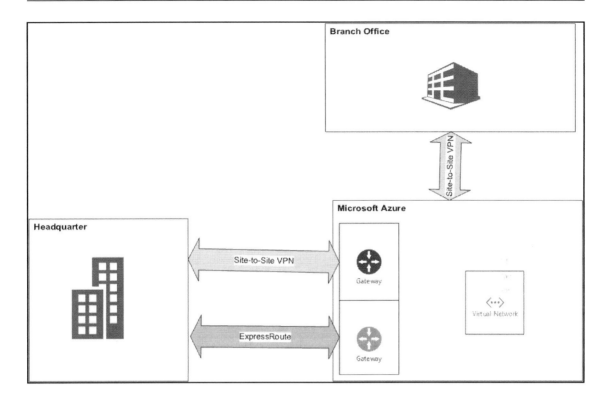

Routing, load balancing, or more general traffic directions

In the last section of the chapter, we dealt with the various aspects of the subject of connectivity, symbolically, the traffic network (or the road network) between the individual corner points of our VNets.

In this section, we will take a step forward and deal with topics such as routing and load balancing, and stay in the picture with traffic planning or traffic control.

The section itself is divided into two parts:

- Some theory about routing and so on
- Three specific offers of the Azure platform (Azure Load Balancer, Azure Traffic Manager, and Azure Application Gateway)

Routing

Let's start with a simple question: What is routing? Routing, in computer science or in telecommunication, means defining paths (or rather more precisely, defining the entire path, including all way-points) for message streams during message transmission in a network.

This is a very general explanation and therefore we should now look at the topic of routing in the area of Azure networking. For Azure networking, packet-switched routing is generally used. This is the same routing method which is also the basis of the internet.

What is packet-switched routing? In packet-switched routing, it is ensured that logically addressed data packets emerge from the originating network and are forwarded to their destination network. The data packets can pass many different intermediate networks on their way to their destination.

To know where packets are to be sent, the structure of the network must be known. In small networks, the information required for routing is easily configured manually. For large networks with very complex topologies, which may change often, capture is often dynamic.

Since routing can only very slowly determine the best paths relative to the number of packets to be moved, the best possible paths are stored in one or more routing tables. Also, Azure networking uses a standard routing table for its work.

Why do I tell you this? Ok so far, it was a general description of how it works. But there are exceptions (or specialties) which I will introduce to you now.

User-defined routes

Although the use of routes automatically allows traffic to be deployed to your deployment, there are cases where you want to control the routing of packets through a virtual appliance (a network virtual appliance).

To do this, you can create custom routes (so-called **user-defined routes**) that specify the next hop for packets to a particular subnet, and specify that the packets should be sent to your virtual application instead.

Custom routes are available only for traffic within or between VNets. It is not possible to use custom routes to traffic from the internet. There is only one restriction that is a custom route can only be created using an ARM template, with Azure PowerShell, or with the Azure CLI.

Routing using the BGP

BGP is the standard routing protocol that is used to exchange routing and presence information between multiple networks on the internet.

In the context of virtual Azure networks, Azure VPN gateways and your local VPN devices (BGP peers or neighbors) can use BGP routes to exchange information about the availability and availability of the prefixes that the involved gateways or routers pass through.

BGP also allows transit routing between multiple networks. For this purpose, determined routes of a BGP peer are passed on to all other BGP peers.

In the Azure networking area, routing with BGP is used with Azure Site-to-Site and Azure ExpressRoute connections.

Azure Load Balancer

Let us clarify the question first: What is the Azure Load Balancer? The Azure Load Balancer is a load distribution module for incoming traffic at layer 4 (OSI Reference Model's transportation layer). It provides the even distribution of network traffic across all instances of an application running in the same Azure Data Center.

Currently, there are two types of load balancers:

- **Internet-facing Load Balancer**: This load balancing module performs the mapping of the incoming data traffic to the private IP addresses and port numbers of the virtual machines and, conversely, also maps the response traffic from the virtual machine to the clients.

The load balancing module requires the following additional resources to perform its tasks:

- **Public IP address**: A public IP address is needed for the load balancer to receive internet traffic
- **Frontend configuration**: This associates the public IP address with the load balancer
- **Backend address pool**: Contains a list of the NICs for all resources that will receive the incoming traffic

Using rules, you can distribute certain types of traffic to multiple virtual machines or services. For example, you can distribute web requests to multiple web servers or web roles.

There are currently two types of rules available:

- **Load balancer rules**: Load balancer rules are used to distribute network traffic among all the resources in the backend address pool
- **Network address translation (NAT) rules**: NAT rules are used to route traffic to a specific resource:
    - ILB: This load balancing module performs the mapping of incoming traffic between Azure resources (such as between VNets)

Unlike the Azure Load Balancer, the ILB requires a private IP address. To give the ILB a private IP address, create a frontend configuration and assign it to the VNet or subnet that they want to address.

There are currently two types of Stock Keeping Units available:

- Azure Load Balancer Basic
- Azure Load Balancer Standard (Preview)

There are actually no differences between the SKUs (the same functionality, the same APIs, and so on), but the Azure Load Balancer Standard works with backend pools up to 1,000 devices (with basic being only 100 devices), and also supports availability zones (simultaneous working in several Azure Regions).

I still have a little candy: the use of the Azure Load Balancer Basic is free.

Azure Traffic Manager

Here is our starting question: What is the Azure Traffic Manager? Like the Azure Load Balancer, the Traffic Manager is a mechanism to distribute incoming traffic among different Azure Data Centers. Unlike the load balancing of the other Azure Balancers, the Traffic Manager's work is based on distribution via DNS entries, which means you deploy a DNS name for the Traffic Manager.

The clients connect directly to the endpoint for the application which has the best response time for its location. The Azure Traffic Manager is, for example, used as a frontend for applications distributed over different Azure regions

Azure Application Gateway

And again, the question: What is the Azure Application Gateway? Azure Application Gateway is an **application delivery controller** (**ADC**) as a service, providing various load balancing functions at layer 7 (OSI Reference Model's application layer). It is highly available, scalable, and fully managed by the Azure platform.

The Azure Application Gateway currently provides the following features:

- **HTTP Load Balancer**: This is a load balancing method based on round robin for HTTP or HTTPS data traffic

    What is round robin? Round robin refers to a scheduling process and allows several competing processes to access the required limited resources one by one for a short period of time. Round robin in the load balancing area exists in two forms:

    - **Load balancing for DNS**: The module makes a request to a name server that provides a list of available IP addresses of the resource. The incoming traffic is then distributed evenly.
    - **Load balancing for routing**: The module ensures that routes with the same node metric and the same target network are loaded in sequence during the package delivery.

- **Cookie-based session affinity**: This ensures that the one user session always remains on the same backend. By using gateway-managed cookies, the Application Gateway can route further traffic from a user session to the same backend for processing.
- **Advanced SSL**:
    - **SSL offload**: With this function, the SSL connection on the Application Gateway is terminated and the traffic is forwarded unencrypted to the server. This results in a discharge of the server. The response of the server is then encrypted again by the Application Gateway before returning it to the client.
    - **End-to-end SSL**: With this function, the SSL connection on the Application Gateway is terminated. Then the defined routing rules are applied to the data traffic, the packet is encrypted again, and finally the packet is forwarded to the corresponding backend based on the routing rules. Replies from the server go through the same process back to the end user.

- **Azure web application firewall (WAF)**: The WAF (based on the Apache ModSecurity module) is an integral part of the Azure Application Gateway and protects your web apps from the most common exploits and security risks. These security problems include, for example, SQL injection, Cross-Site Scripting, and session hijacking.

 The Azure WAF is based on the **Open Web Application Security Project (OWASP)** core rule set. You can find more information here: `https://www.owasp.org/index.php/Category:OWASP_ModSecurity_Core_Rule_Set_Project.`

- Routing from application requests to an HTTP listener
- Support for WebSockets
- Support for application pools

 If you want to integrate an Azure Application Gateway into your VNet, you need a separate subnet for the deployment.

Security

If we are dealing with the subject of Azure networking, we must not forget the area of security.

As a tool for this, Azure networking offers the following options:

- NSG
- Application security groups

NSG

An NSG contains a list of rules that allow or deny network traffic for resources associated with VNets.

Currently, there are the following types of NSGs:

- NSG applied to a NIC
- NSG applied to a subnet
- NSG applied to a VM (only available in a classical deployment)

If an NSG is associated with a subnet, the rules apply to all resources that are connected to the subnet. However, you can further restrict your data traffic by setting up NSGs for NICs or VMs.

An NSG cannot be used concurrently with an endpoint **access control list** (**ACL**). We come next to the keyword **rules**, or rather **NSG rules**. In principle, rules are offered in two categories, namely rules for incoming traffic and rules for outgoing traffic. As an action for all rules, only the following operations are possible: allow traffic – deny traffic.

Let's look at the NSG rules in more detail. An NSG rule consists of the following properties:

Property	Description	Constraints
Name	Name for the rule.	Must be unique within the region. Can contain letters, numbers, underscores, periods, and hyphens.
Protocol	Protocol to match for the rule.	TCP, UDP, or *.
Source port range	Source port range to match for the rule.	Single port number, port range, or * (for all ports).
Destination port range	Destination port range to match for the rule.	Single port number, port range, or * (for all ports).
Source address prefix	Source address prefix or tag to match for the rule.	Single IP address, IP subnet, or * (for all addresses).
Destination address prefix	Destination address prefix or tag to match for the rule.	Single IP address, IP subnet, or * (for all addresses).
Direction	Direction of traffic to match for the rule.	Inbound or outbound.

Priority	Rules are checked in the order of priority. Once a rule applies, no more rules are tested for matching.	Number between 100 and 4,096.
Access	Type of access to apply if the rule matches.	Allow or deny.

All NSGs contain a set of standard rules after creation. The default rules cannot be deleted, but have the lowest priority and can be overridden by self-created rules.

The standard rules allow or deny data traffic:

- **Virtual network**: Data traffic is allowed from or to a virtual network in the incoming and outgoing direction.
- **Internet**: Outgoing traffic is allowed. Incoming traffic is blocked.
- **Load balancing**: Allow Azure to check the integrity of the virtual machines and the role instances. You can override this rule if you do not use load balancing.

There are limits for the use of NSGs and NSG rules: Only 100 NSGs and 200 NSG rules (per NSG) are currently allowed per subscription.

Application security groups

An Application security group is a natural extension of an NSG to an application architecture. The basis for this is the grouping of virtual computers (VMs). The network security guidelines are then assigned to these groups.

The Application security groups feature has been new since the Microsoft Ignite 2017 Conference (September 2017) and currently has preview status.

Security infrastructure

While a network security group provides a certain degree of network security on the switching and transport level of the OSI Reference Model, situations may arise in which you want to enable security for the higher levels of the stack.

In these situations, it is advisable to provide appliances provided by Azure partners for the security of virtual networks. These solutions are called Network Virtual Appliances (C).

NVA

Let's start with the question: What is an NVA? The answer consists of several parts as follows:

- An NVA is usually a third-party solution and is distributed over the Azure Marketplace
- An NVA is offered in the form of a VM
- An NVA is part of its own VNet subnet and stands apart from the rest of the VNet

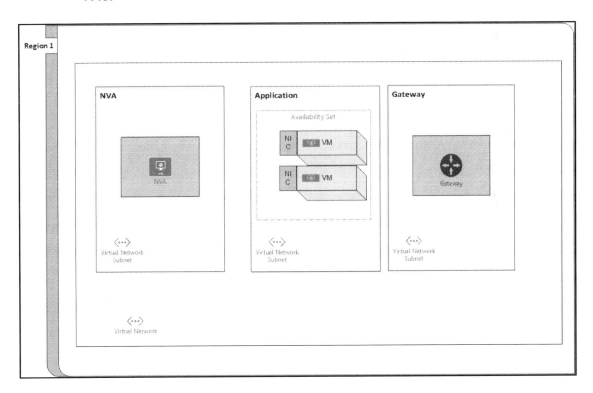

Examples of using a NVA are:

- Firewall
- Intrusion detection/intrusion prevention
- Management of security risks
- Application control
- Network-based detection of anomalies
- Web filtering
- Virus protection
- Bot protection

One example of using an NVA in a VNet architecture, is to set up a DMZ using firewall solutions, such as offered by Barracuda, Palo Alto, Fortinet or Sophos.

Management and monitoring

Let's go to the last topic of our round trip in the area of Azure networking, management, and monitoring.

For this, the Azure platform provides you with the following portfolio:

- **Microsoft OMS**: The OMS is a cloud-based solution that combines the management of your cloud environments, with the capabilities of the System Center (SC 2016).
- **Azure Monitor**: Azure Monitor is an Azure service for monitoring and diagnosing Azure resources. However, you need to know that Azure Monitor generally accesses existing (and thus old) management capabilities of the Azure platform. These capabilities are, however, first brought together in a common GUI, the Azure Monitor.
- **Azure Network Watcher**: The Azure Network Watcher is a service that allows you to monitor and diagnose conditions at the level of network scenarios in Azure. The included tools for network diagnostics and visualization help you understand your network in Azure, perform diagnostics, and gain insights.

We will discuss these topics in detail in Chapter 7, *Monitoring and Telemetry*.

Summary

In this chapter, I gave you an overview of Azure networking. First, I presented you with the anatomy of a VNet, and the network elements that occur. Then, in the second part, there was a deep dive into some parts of it (such as connectivity, routing, and more).

In the next chapter, we will end our tour through the Azure platform and begin to deal with specific architectural aspects. We will start with the topic, *Availability*.

5
Availability

In the last four chapters, I have tried to give you a deeper insight into the Azure platform with a comprehensive introduction. You have learned which building blocks (services) are available and how they can be used (also, of course, combining individual parts with each other). At least theoretically, you know all the basics to create your own Azure solutions.

Or? Yes, if I ask, there is, of course, an *or*.

I am a solution architect, which means I construct individual solutions for enterprises. The process of designing an enterprise application is very complex, and knowing the available components is only one part of this process. So, if we want to look at the design process as a whole, we also have to consider the aspect of everyday work, along with the solution.

What are the aspects of daily work? Answering this question is a bit difficult, as there is usually no clear picture of what we consider relevant to our work. In order to provide at least one approach to an answer, I have a few examples:

- Availability
- Performance
- Monitoring and telemetry
- Security and some more

In this chapter, we will take a closer look at some aspects of this list. We will start with the topic availability.

I still have one important point—the area's availability and performance are similar in some ways. One aspect that is important for availability can also be significant for performance.

We will explore, in detail, the following topics in this chapter:

- What is availability?
- Uptime and downtime
- **Service Level Agreement (SLA)**
- Planned maintenance
- Azure autoscaling

What is availability?

Actually, a simple question but the answer is very complex. So, in turn, look into the following approaches.

First approach

Availability is the ratio of time within an agreed period in which the system is operational for its actual purpose (operation time) at the agreed time.

The operating time may be limited by:

- Planned maintenance
- Unplanned maintenance
- Error
- Damage
- Repair time to eliminate errors and damage

The measure of availability is usually given as a percentage.

Second approach

Alternatively, availability is also defined as the proportion of available objects (services) in the total number of objects (services). In summary, availability is thus a quality criterion and a measure for a system, subsystem, service, and so on. So, now you know what availability means. In the following sections, we will concentrate on the first approach presented.

Uptime and downtime

Before we go further into the details, we still need to clarify two terms that are important to our explanation:

- Uptime
- Downtime

The term, *uptime*, is easily explained, it is just another name for what I mentioned in the previous section of the chapter, operation time. In other words, the period of time when an application runs without errors and without interruptions.

The term, *downtime*, then designates as a counterpart, the period where it comes to an interruption. However, it does not matter to us whether the disruption has been deliberately caused (for example, in the case of maintenance tasks), or is a consequence of errors, damage or even a total failure.

Why are these terms important to us? Both values are part of the calculation of the degree of availability, and thus also a part of the definition of a SLA.

SLA

Although the term, SLA has already been mentioned, the first question is what is an SLA? Although there are several answers (any infrastructure architect among you can confirm that), I would like to confine myself to the following simple answer:

An SLA is a contract between you and your cloud service provider that guarantees you a certain degree of availability for services booked. That sounds very good, but in real life that just means that you get your money back if the guarantee is not respected.

Nevertheless, we should now pursue the question: how do I determine a degree of availability? For the degree of availability, we first need the desired uptime. This can vary according to your needs. For example, if you operate a webshop, the targeted uptime is 24 hours x 7 days or 168 hours per week or 8,760 hours per year. But if you only have one application for the daily work in your company, the desired uptime can be limited to a core time, for example, 100 hours per week or 5,200 hours per year.

Let's now proceed to the calculation—take the desired uptime value, subtract a downtime value, and divide the result again by the uptime value used. Then multiply the value by 100 and you have a value for the degree of availability.

Here is an example calculation:
8,760 hours uptime – 1 hour downtime/8,760 hours x 100 = 99.99. The degree of availability is *99.99 %*.

As I wrote earlier, the SLA includes a guaranteed availability degree. This is usually between 99.95 % and 99.99 % for Microsoft Azure. For us, this means a possible downtime between 53 minutes and 43 hours, 20 minutes.

 A service with an availability degree of at least 99% is referred to as high availability.

Also, it is important to know that Microsoft grants an SLA only if you have at least two instances of your service.

 You can find a list of available SLAs here: `https://azure.microsoft.com/en-us/support/legal/sla/`.

Some extra information about SLAs, in addition to the availability level, the following key metrics are often specified:

- **Mean time to recovery (MTTR)**: This means the duration of recovery after a failure
- **Mean time between failures (MTBF)**: This is the average operating time between two occurring errors without repair time
- **Mean time to failure (MTTF)**: This metric is used when components are not repaired but replaced

Now I have taught you enough theory. Let's now dedicate ourselves to practical work with an SLA.

I have two concepts for this. The first offer is the so-called SLA management pattern and, at least for the Azure platform, is of a rather theoretical nature, since there is no example of a practical implementation.

What is it about? Quite simply, every action that any consumer takes against a cloud service is registered by an **SLA Monitor Agent** and recorded as a log entry in a **Quality of Service (QoS)** repository (a data store). The repository then transmits the data to an SLA management service and the SLA management service acts as a reporting tool for **Cloud Admin**, as shown here:

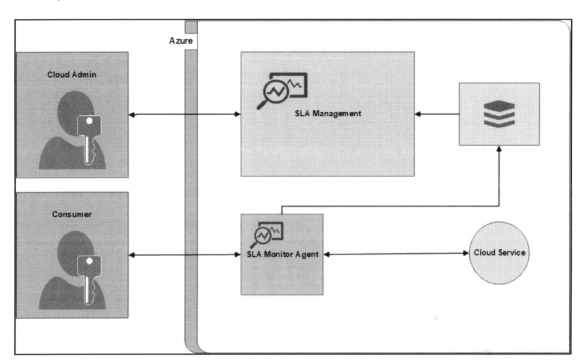

What is the issue with this solution? There are no ready-made offers available on the Azure platform. So, you have to develop them yourself or buy third-party components.

Is this solution too complex for you? Then I would like to introduce you to a more practical way. The procedure is known by software architects as the Health Endpoint Monitoring pattern.

What is it about? To guarantee the availability of your application, it is advisable to carry out an access test at regular intervals. This should be done through shared endpoints (but you should create an additional endpoint for the tests and not use the default endpoint), or talk to a test page in the case of a web application.

Let's take a closer look:

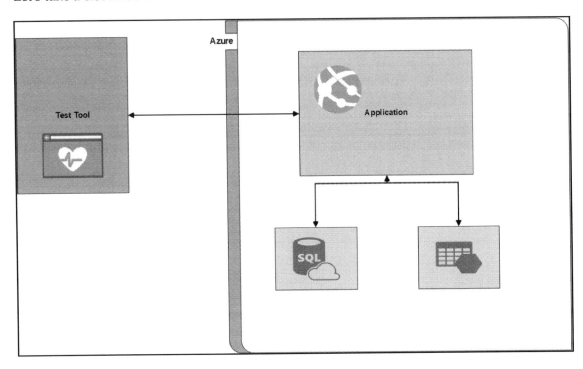

As shown in the preceding diagram, the test tool sends a request to the application at regular intervals. If the application is available, it responds with an HTTP 200 code (ok). If the application is not available, you get an HTTP 404 code (not found) instead.

In the same way, you can also check the availability of downstream services (for example, Azure SQL Database or Azure Storage).

  An example of the Health Endpoint Monitoring pattern in code form can be found here: `https://github.com/mspnp/cloud-design-patterns/tree/master/health-endpoint-monitoring`.

What's the issue with this solution? Depending on the complexity of your Azure solutions, you need to extend the example with your own developments (for example, a TCP check for TCP/IP endpoints).

Planned maintenance

Let's get to the area of planned maintenance. This is the only predictable downtime (usually twice a year) on the Azure platform.

Planned maintenance is used to install necessary updates on the platform or for general maintenance, and can have an effect on all of your Azure IaaS deployments (such as Azure VM), or on all of your Azure PaaS solutions based on an Azure VM, (such as Azure Service Fabric).

What are the effects?

Here, I first have to take a small step backward. The majority of planned maintenance will not affect the operations of the platform (for example, storage infrastructure updates or physical network infrastructure updates).

With other updates that affect your VMs directly, things look different. This includes the following:

- Host security and compliance patching
- Updates for the Azure host agents
- Updates for the network agents
- HW decommissioning
- HW maintenance
- Host OS rollout

Since each of these updates places specific requirements on the platform, two subtypes of planned maintenance have evolved:

- **VM preserving maintenance (also known as preserving host updates)**: The VM is placed in a **Paused** state, and will be resumed within 30 seconds. Used memory, network connection, and open files are kept in their respective state. The maintenance type, VM preserving maintenance, is used for updates in the areas of host security and compliance patching, Azure host agents and network agents.

- **VM restarting maintenance**: Basically, this type of maintenance has one thing in common. Each affected VM will be rebooted in some way. Nevertheless, there are two subtypes here:
  - **VM reboot**: The VM will be restarted. The state of memory, network connections, and open files are lost.
  - **VM redeploy**: The VM is moved to another host. The state of memory, network connections, open files and the transient drive info are lost.

The maintenance type, VM restarting maintenance, is used for updates in the areas of HW decommissioning, HW maintenance, and host OS rollouts.

Best practice: Although Microsoft is currently trying to simplify the planned maintenance process for the customer (for example, a VM restart event is not scheduled to happen more than once a year), you should secure your applications by letting it run on at least two instances at the same time.

As I've already written, planned maintenance is the only predictable downtime. For many, the question arises of how do I do that?

Here is some brief guidance:

1. Open your Azure management portal at `https://portal.azure.com`.
2. In the navigation area of the portal, click on **Help + support**.
3. This opens the **Help + support** dashboard, as shown in the following screenshot. In the navigation area of the dashboard, click on **Planned maintenance**.
4. If a scheduled maintenance is pending, you can see it in the now open list (**No maintenance events are scheduled**):

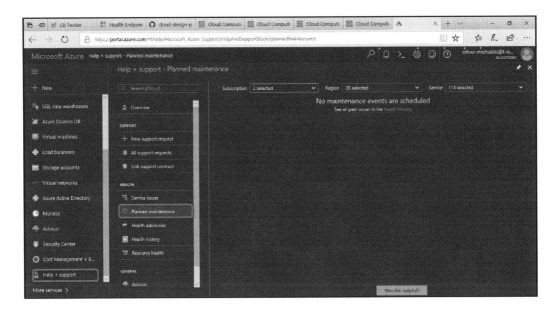

It is important to know that you do not need to visit the **Help + support** dashboard regularly to avoid planned maintenance. Thirty days before a planned maintenance, you will also receive a notification about the platform's notification service, as shown in the following screenshot:

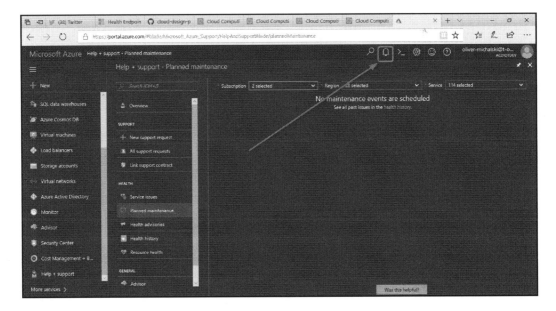

Here is an anecdote to end with and maybe a reason to think carefully about the issue. In February 2012, it was part of a planned maintenance to import a faulty update (the update had the leap year excluded). The result? The operation of most of the Azure data center was canceled for a long time.

However, I do not want to end my remarks without at least once going into the second approach of availability definition. There is an interesting solution for this, which I will introduce to you now.

Azure autoscaling

Once again, remember that availability can also be defined as the proportion of available objects (services) in the total number of objects (services).

Immediately the question arises, does the availability rate increase as the number of available objects increases and if so, how do I achieve this? To answer the question, yes.

It increases the level of availability, and with the Azure autoscaling feature, there is also a platform-based way to do it.

Scaling is a complex topic because it can occur in two ways. With vertical scaling, I do not increase the number of instances of a service but migrate the service to the next higher performance level. With horizontal scaling instead, I increase the rule-based number of instances.

In summary, while vertical scaling only influences the performance of your application, horizontal scaling can also affect the availability of the application.

Let's take a closer look at horizontal scaling. As I've already written, horizontal scaling is rule-based. But to be honest, that's just part of the reality. Before the autoscale engine can work, you need a complete configuration called autoscale settings, which consists of more than just rules.

Just take a look at the following diagram:

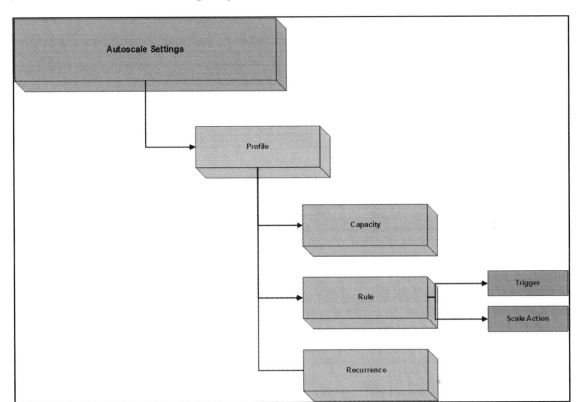

What can you see? The highest element of the configuration is the so-called **Autoscale Settings**. An autoscale setting is read by the autoscale engine to determine how to scale.

The autoscale settings contain one or more profiles. An autoscale profile is a combination of:

- **Capacity settings**: Capacity settings specify the minimum, maximum, and default values for the number of instances
- **Rules**: Each rule includes a trigger (time or metric) and a scale action (up or down)
- **Recurrence**: Recurrence indicates when the autoscale engine should put a profile into effect

Let's go back to the topic of rules. As you have read, a rule contains a trigger (an action) that triggers scaling. The trigger is based on either a timestamp (for example, Saturdays at 6:00 PM) or a metric (for example, CPU usage).

Metrics are usually provided by the Azure Monitor service. For a list of available metrics for the autoscaling section, see the following table:

Metric name	Unit
\Processor(_Total)% Processor Time	Percent
\Processor(_Total)% Privileged Time	Percent
\Processor(_Total)% User Time	Percent
\Processor Information(_Total)\Processor Frequency	Count
\System\Processes	Count
\Process(_Total)\Thread Count	Count
\Process(_Total)\Handle Count	Count
\Memory% Committed Bytes In Use	Percent
\Memory\Available Bytes	Bytes
\Memory\Committed Bytes	Bytes
\Memory\Commit Limit	Bytes
\Memory\Pool Paged Bytes	Bytes
\Memory\Pool Nonpaged Bytes	Bytes
\PhysicalDisk(_Total)% Disk Time	Percent
\PhysicalDisk(_Total)% Disk Read Time	Percent
\PhysicalDisk(_Total)% Disk Write Time	Percent
\PhysicalDisk(_Total)\Disk Transfers/sec	CountPerSecond
\PhysicalDisk(_Total)\Disk Reads/sec	CountPerSecond
\PhysicalDisk(_Total)\Disk Writes/sec	CountPerSecond
\PhysicalDisk(_Total)\Disk Bytes/sec	BytesPerSecond
\PhysicalDisk(_Total)\Disk Read Bytes/sec	BytesPerSecond
\PhysicalDisk(_Total)\Disk Write Bytes/sec	BytesPerSecond
\PhysicalDisk(_Total)\Avg. Disk Queue Length	Count
\PhysicalDisk(_Total)\Avg. Disk Read Queue Length	Count

`\PhysicalDisk(_Total)\Avg. Disk Write Queue Length`	Count
`\LogicalDisk(_Total)% Free Space`	Percent
`\LogicalDisk(_Total)\Free Megabytes`	Count

Where can I use autoscaling? Currently, autoscaling is available as a built-in option for the following services:

- Azure Cloud Services
- Azure Service Fabric (scaling of SF clusters)
- Azure App Services (without Azure Functions)
- Azure VMs

Azure Functions (actually a part of Azure App Services) does not need the autoscaling build-in option because it scales automatically when needed. The autoscaling build-in option on Azure VMs is a special case because they only work in a so-called VM Scale Set.

A VM Scale Set can, by default, contain up to 100 identical VMs. But if you set the `singlePlacementGroup` property to `false` when you create the VM Scale Set, you can use up to 1,000 identical VMs.

With the help of autoscaling, you now have the option to automatically add VMs to your scale set until the limits are reached. The deployment takes place within a few minutes.

Summary

In this chapter, we started with an insight into specific architecture aspects that are important for the daily use of the Azure platform and are part of the design process for your own Azure solutions. The main topic we focused on was availability. You have learned the basics and direct references to the Azure platform (for example, in the case of planned maintenance).

In the next chapter, we will continue with our series on special architecture aspects, this time with a focus on performance and scalability.

6
Performance and Scalability

After an in-depth look at the Azure platform in the first four chapters, I started in the last chapter to expand our viewpoint on special architectural aspects that influence our daily work, and thus also the design process for our own Azure solutions.

The first topic we examined was the aspect of availability. Now we will expand this area and also look at the aspect of performance (and again the aspect of scalability).

To be clear, the issues of availability and performance go together; they are, strictly speaking, the two sides of the same coin. On the one hand, you are asked how many machines are available and, on the other hand, how strong or powerful these machines are.

The third theme, scalability, is then just a means to an end. How do I get more machines? How can I get more performance from my machine?

We will explore the following topics in detail in this chapter:

- What is performance?
- Service level objectives
- Analyzing and interpreting performance data
- Scaling

What is performance?

Let's start with a simple answer: performance is a unit of mass for data processing speed (in other words, for the number of calculations in a given period of time). Performance is measured at the system level (*system performance*) or determined for individual parts of the computer (for example, CPU performance or **graphics processing unit** (**GPU**) performance).

If that were the answer, we could stop now, but unfortunately, the situation in real life is not that easy.

As software architects, we are not, or are only marginally, interested in the system's performance. Instead, we are interested in the performance of our application (application performance) and it depends on several factors.

This includes the following:

- The code base of your application
- The performance of the underlying Azure services (components performance)

Regarding performances of the Azure services, the initial situation is more complicated for us because there are no uniform criteria for the performance terms.

Some examples are as follows:

Azure VMs and all services based on Azure VMs (Azure Cloud Service, Azure Container Service, Azure Service Fabric). Here, you set the performance level by selecting an Azure series. Which Azure series you choose depends on your individual workload and your specific requirements.

An Azure series (also known as VM type or VM instance) generally differs in the number of CPU cores, the amount of memory, and the maximum size of the data disk. Some Azure series or individual parts of it are also defined by special hardware.

Microsoft offers the following Azure series:

- **A-series**: The A-series supports the full feature scope of Azure VMs for a wide range of workloads.
- **A-series (Basic)**: A light version of the A-series (only available for instances A0 –A4), designed for development and testing starter workloads.
- **A-series (compute intensive)**: A high-end version of the A-series, designed for high-performance computing and data-intensive workloads (video encoding, for example). The series includes **high-throughput network interfaces (RDMA)** as an option.
- **A-series version 2 (Av2-series)**: Series Av2 is the latest generation of the A-series and specifically designed for Azure DevTest Lab scenarios or for use as an Azure Service Fabric (a microservice architecture). With series Av2, the performance for data access is significantly higher, since only **Solid State Drives (SSD)** are used for data storage.

- **B-series**: B-series is intended for workloads that do not require full CPU performance continuously, such as web servers, or development and test environments.

Each instance of the BS-series provides a basic level (minimum value) for performance and then has the capability of extending to 100% CPU utilization of an Intel® Broadwell E5-2673 v4 2.3GHz or an Intel® Haswell 2.4 GHz E5-2673 v3 processor. As long as you use less than the basic performance with the VM instance, you acquire a credit balance. As soon as you are in credit, you can also use the performance that goes beyond the basic level.

All you have to do is to answer the question, which basic level best suits my needs?

- **D-series and DS-series**: D-series VMs are designed to run applications that demand higher compute power and temporary disk performance. To achieve this, a D-series VM provides a better processor performance and a higher memory-to-core ratio, and an SSD is used for the temporary disk.
- **D and DS-series version 2 (Dv2-series and DSv2-series)**: Dv2-series and DSv2-series are the next generations of the D-series and DS-series. Dv2-series and DSv2-series are identical to the original series but have a 35% higher CPU performance based on the Intel Xeon® E5-2673 v3 (Haswell) processor.
- **D-series and DS-series version 3 (Dv3 and Dsv3)**: Dv3-series and Dsv3-series are the latest generations of the D-series and DS-series. Dv3-series and Dsv3-series are based on the Intel® Broadwell E5-2673 v4 2.3GHz processor, or the Intel® Haswell 2.4 GHz E5-2673 v3 processor and introduce Hyper-Threading Technology and **virtual CPUs (vCPUs)** as key architectural elements. The new series provides also some of the first VMs to be running on a Windows Server 2016 host. Windows 2016 hosts enable nested virtualization and Hyper-V containers for these new instances. Nested virtualization allows you to run a Hyper-V server on an Azure VM.
- **E-series and ES-series version 3 (Ev3-series and ESv3-series)**: The Ev3-series and ESv3-series are also part of the latest generation of the D-series and DS-series, and the new name for the high-memory instances D11-D14. For the Ev3-series and ESv3-series, the same description applies as for the Dv3-series and Dsv3-series.
- **F-series and Fs-series**: F-series and Fs-series offer a high CPU-to-RAM ratio, ideal for web servers, network appliances, batch processing, and medium-load application servers or real-time communication.

- **FS-series version 2 (Fsv2-series)**: The Fsv2-series is the next generation of the Fs-series. The Fsv2-series are based on the fastest Intel® Xeon® Scalable processor, code-named Skylake (Intel® Xeon® Platinum 8168 processor), and featuring a base core frequency of 2.7 GHz and a maximum single-core turbo frequency of 3.7 GHz. Fsv2-series provides the Hyper-Threading Technology and the Intel® **Advanced Vector Extensions (AVX)** 512 instructions set, as key architectural elements.

- **G-series and GS-series**: The G-series and GS-series are a clone of the older D-series and DS-series, but the G-series instances have a memory twice as large, and temporary disks based on an SSD that are four times larger. With exceptional, high-performance VM sizes in the G range, you can easily handle business critical applications such as large relational database servers (SQL Server, MySQL, and so on) or large NoSQL databases (MongoDB, Cloudera Cassandra, and so on).

- **H-series:** The H-series is designed for high-performance computing and data-intensive workloads (for example, molecular modeling and flow dynamics). The series includes **high-throughput network interfaces (RDMA)** as an option.

- **Ls-series:** The Ls-series is a clone of the GS-series and built for low latency storage requirements greater the offerings of the GS-series.

- **M Series:** The M-series offers the highest number of CPUs (up to 128 vCPUs) and the largest memory (up to 2.0 TB) for a virtual machine on the Azure platform. This is ideal for extremely large databases or other high-end applications that require a high CPU count and large amounts of memory.

- **N-series:** The N-series is not defined by factors such as CPU or memory, but by the ability to use **GPUs** (the processors of the graphics card) as an additional power factor. Additional computing capacity is provided in the form of the GPU, whereby the GPU generally operates faster than the CPU in highly parallelizable program sequences (high data parallelism), and therefore, a simple way is sought to supplement the computing performance of CPUs by the computing performance of GPUs. The **Compute Unified Device Architecture (CUDA)** and/or **Open Computing Language (OpenCL)** technologies are used for this purpose. The use of the GPU performance is particularly suitable for computers and graphics with intensive workloads and supports you in scenarios such as high-end visualization, deep learning, and predictive analytics.

As you can see, there are some Azure series that have an *S* within the name. Those series VMs use SSDs and Azure Premium Storage as the primary storage type for data and operating systems.

Even if you have decided on an Azure series, you can change this decision at any time after deployment.

Azure SQL Database: Again, you can choose between different options with the decisive difference that the underlying definition follows a different approach.

How is an Azure SQL Database performance level defined? A performance level is defined by the number of permitted **Database Transaction Units** (**DTUs**). The second criterion formerly used, the so-called transaction rate (a metric from the **Azure SQL Database Benchmark** (**ASDB**) to capture the maximum transaction throughput per hour, minute, or second) will no longer be used.

What is a DTU?

DTU is a bit difficult, as it can be described as an object, but it is not actually a real object. DTUs are performance units to which a certain percentage of the total performance of the database server is allocated in CPU, memory, and read or write rates. The offered performance levels contain between 5 DTU (in the Basic service level) and 4,000 DTUs (in the Premium service level P15).

The larger the number of DTUs, the greater the performance of the database. Another criterion for the selection of a performance level is the maximum size of the database.

Also, the maximum size, that can reach the database depends on the selected performance level. The maximum size of the database per level is:

- **Basic**: 2 GB
- **Standard (S0 – S12)**: 250 GB
- **Premium (P1 – P6)**: 500 GB
- **Premium (P11 + P15)**: 4 TB
- **Premium RS**: 500 GB

Is that all now? No, also the number of simultaneously concurrent requests (maximum concurrent workers), the number of concurrent logins (maximum concurrent logins), and the number of concurrent sessions (maximum sessions) are limited per level.

As you can see, performance depends on many factors when using Azure services. Here are the most important ones:

- CPU selection (number of CPUs, number of cores, processor type)
- RAM
- Memory (maximum size)
- Memory for temporary data (maximum size, SSD or HDD)
- Use of the GPU (graphics card processor)
- Latency
- **Input/output operations per second (IOPS)**

Service level objectives

In the last chapter, I tried to introduce you to the topic of **service level agreement (SLA)**. An SLA is a contract that includes a guaranteed value for the availability. In addition to this guaranteed value, so-called **service level objectives (SLOs)** can also be used. But SLOs are not guarantees, but goals in the performance area. In other words, the service is just trying to reach a certain level. The entire environment and interaction with other services can have a negative impact.

Typical SLOs can be found in the following areas:

- **Throughput**: How many operations can be performed in a given period of time?
- **Concurrency**: How many operations can be performed simultaneously?
- **Latency**: How long does the system take to perform an operation?
- **Headroom**: How much capacity does the system have to allow growth?
- **Error rate**: How many exceptions does the system generate while performing operations?

 SLOs are also called **Key Performance Indicators (KPIs)**.

Now we have learned a lot of theory about performance. But we also want to work in this area. For example, we want to know: where does a bottleneck exist in my application?

Analyzing and interpreting performance data

Now we want to integrate the subject of performance into our daily work. What do we have to do to achieve this goal? There is a simple answer: a lot of planning. In other words, we need to find the answers that suit the following questions.

What are our business workloads?

Now you might think, I operate (for example) an e-commerce application. What is this question about? There is a simple answer: the operation of the e-commerce application is only the highest level, in fact, the process comprises at least the following workloads:

- Identifying customers
- Registering new customers
- Browsing products
- Placing orders
- Status of orders
- All administrative tasks such as maintaining the product catalog or generating month-end reports

Why is knowledge about existing business workloads important to us?

Each of these workloads can have a different usage pattern, and each pattern can vary depending on external circumstances.

For instance, browsing products is likely to be the most commonly performed operation, followed by placing orders. The performance requirements for these operations can peak at certain times of the day and then subside. Also, other circumstances, such as the introduction of a new, emerging product, may cause high demand for resources for a short period of time.

Now we know what workloads we have. The question that arises is what's next? Next, we need to be clear about our performance goals. Clarity about performance goals means:

- What performance requirements do I need or should strive for?
- What performance characteristics does the system (the service) offer to meet these requirements?

Unfortunately, the answer to these questions depends on your individual needs, so I cannot go into them further.

What are we still missing?

Before we start working, we should also look at the tools. What tools are there and for what use are they intended? The following list gives you an overview of the currently available offer:

- **Azure management portal**: The Azure portals provide dashboards that display specific metrics for Azure services that might not be available through APM tools or profilers. You can view, for example, the average latency of Azure Storage, or the rate for messaging within an Azure IoT Hub.
- **System specific tools**: Some services (including third-party services) frequently provide their own monitoring and analysis utilities. Examples include the SQL management views, and the **Query Performance** page in the SQL Management Studio. These tools are dependent on the nature of the service being provided. For example, the **Query Performance** page in the SQL Management Studio lets you view the details of the query execution plan for recently executed SQL statements. If you have an understanding of how SQL Server optimizes queries, you might be able to use this information to make your queries more efficient.
- **Performance counters**: Performance counters refers to the measured values which are captured by the Windows operating system. A large number of different counters are available. However, many of them only record data at a low level, such as the counter for speed at which drives are read or written, the counter for memory available on the computer, or the counter for the CPU load of an application. These metrics are gathered automatically and the collection process is transparent to applications and services. Services can also create their own custom counters. For example, ASP.NET adds counters that track the request queue length and the rate at which requests are sent and responses received. Tools such as Windows Performance Monitor can be used to visualize performance counters. Applications and services may use them to trigger alerts if they stray outside an expected range. However, the performance counters only use sampling, so it is possible that one or more significant outliers could be missed.

Since you cannot use the Windows Performance Monitor directly on the Azure platform, you have the option to use the data via the Azure Monitor and/or Azure Application Insights.

- **Log parser**: Applications and services can generate their own custom diagnostic trace information and record it to log files (for examples the IIS Log, the Windows Event Log, or custom files created by applications for logging purposes). The data is typically text-based, but the format of the data might vary significantly from file to file. A log parser lets you quickly read and process the contents of different log files. You can also use it to perform analyses, for example, sorting and aggregating log records and filters. The protocol parser uses SQL-like syntax to specify queries about log data.

You can find a Log Parser here: `https://www.microsoft.com/en-us/download/details.aspx?id=24659`.

- **Profilers**: These tools provide a granular view of how an individual executable is consuming resources, enabling you to perform in-depth investigations into CPU, memory, disk, network, garbage collection, and threading. Most of these tools are based on **Event Tracing for Windows** (**ETW**), so they can be used to track and analyze code running on any version of Windows. A common feature of these tools is the ability to examine crash and memory dumps to help determine the cause of exceptions. Examples include ANTS Profiler and Visual Studio Profiler (for general application profiling), PerfView (for tracking CPU and memory-related issues), CLR Profiler (for tracking managed memory use), and Concurrency Visualizer.

You can find PerfView here: `https://www.microsoft.com/en-us/download/details.aspx?id=28567`. You can find the CLR Profiler here: `https://github.com/MicrosoftArchive/clrprofiler`.

- **APM tools**: APM tools are tools that can be used to monitor cloud applications. The capabilities of these tools are not limited to development and testing scenarios but are also used in monitoring production environments. APM tools are designed to minimize the administrative burden of using intelligent strategies, such as the automatic detection of dependent services. APM tools typically use monitoring techniques that do not involve the insertion of code probes. In fact, APM tools rely on system or runtime-provided trace capabilities and autonomous monitoring agents to capture operational data. Examples include Azure Application Insights and the third-party offerings from AppDynamics and New Relic.

 You can find more information about AppDynamics here: `https://www.appdynamics.com/product/application-performance-management/`. You can find more information about New Relics here: `https://newrelic.com/`.

I think that's enough for now. Detailed information on these and other tools can be found in the next chapter.

Scaling

Scaling is a complex topic because it can occur in two ways. With vertical scaling, I do not increase the number of instances of a service but migrate the service to the next higher-performance level. With horizontal scaling instead, I increase the number of instances.

The area scaling is covered on the Azure platform by the so-called **Azure Autoscaling**. Azure Autoscaling is one of the capabilities of the **Azure Monitor service** and works on a **rule-based** basis.

Let's take a closer look. I have already written that scaling is rule-based. But to be honest, that's just part of the reality. Before the autoscale engine can work, you need a complete configuration called **Autoscale Settings**, which consists of more than just rules.

Take a look at the following diagram:

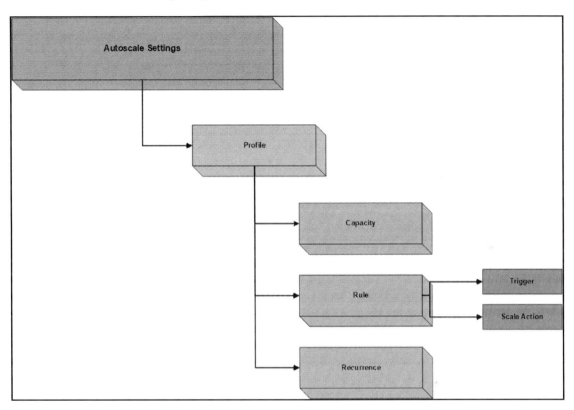

What can you see?

The highest element of the configuration is the so-called Autoscale Settings. An Autoscale Setting is read by the **autoscale engine** to determine how to scale.

The Autoscale Settings contain one or more profiles. An autoscale profile is a combination of the following:

- **Capacity settings**: Capacity settings specify the minimum, maximum, and default values for the number of instances
- **Rule:** Each rule includes a **Trigger** (time or metric) and a **Scale Action** (up or down)
- **Recurrence:** This indicates when the autoscale engine should put a profile into effect

Let's go back to the topic of rules. As you have read, a rule contains a trigger (an action) that triggers scaling. The trigger is either based on a timestamp (for example, Saturday at 6:00 PM), on a metric (for example, CPU usage), or any combination of both.

Most metrics are typically provided by the **Azure Monitor Common Metrics Pool**. For the autoscale section, these are the following metrics:

Metric Name	Unit
`\Processor(_Total)% Processor Time`	Percent
`\Processor(_Total)% Privileged Time`	Percent
`\Processor(_Total)% User Time`	Percent
`\Processor Information(_Total)\Processor Frequency`	Count
`\System\Processes`	Count
`\Process(_Total)\Thread Count`	Count
`\Process(_Total)\Handle Count`	Count
`\Memory% Committed Bytes In Use`	Percent
`\Memory\Available Bytes`	Bytes
`\Memory\Committed Bytes`	Bytes
`\Memory\Commit Limit`	Bytes
`\Memory\Pool Paged Bytes`	Bytes
`\Memory\Pool Nonpaged Bytes`	Bytes
`\PhysicalDisk(_Total)% Disk Time`	Percent
`\PhysicalDisk(_Total)% Disk Read Time`	Percent

\PhysicalDisk(_Total)% Disk Write Time	Percent
\PhysicalDisk(_Total)\Disk Transfers/sec	CountPerSecond
\PhysicalDisk(_Total)\Disk Reads/sec	CountPerSecond
\PhysicalDisk(_Total)\Disk Writes/sec	CountPerSecond
\PhysicalDisk(_Total)\Disk Bytes/sec	BytesPerSecond
\PhysicalDisk(_Total)\Disk Read Bytes/sec	BytesPerSecond
\PhysicalDisk(_Total)\Disk Write Bytes/sec	BytesPerSecond
\PhysicalDisk(_Total)\Avg. Disk Queue Length	Count
\PhysicalDisk(_Total)\Avg. Disk Read Queue Length	Count
\PhysicalDisk(_Total)\Avg. Disk Write Queue Length	Count
\LogicalDisk(_Total)% Free Space	Percent
\LogicalDisk(_Total)\Free Megabytes	Count

If there is no suitable metric, you also have the ability to use your own self-developed metrics for your applications (**custom metrics**). For example, with such a metric you can react to the usage of a shopping cart in a web shop application.

Best practice
When defining a rule for a scale-up process, you should also set a suitable rule for a scale-down process at the same time.

Now I have to clarify something--the horizontal scaling works on the basis of the defined rules. But what if I need vertical scaling?

For the answer, let's go back to the diagram of Autoscale Settings and expand it as shown in the following diagram:

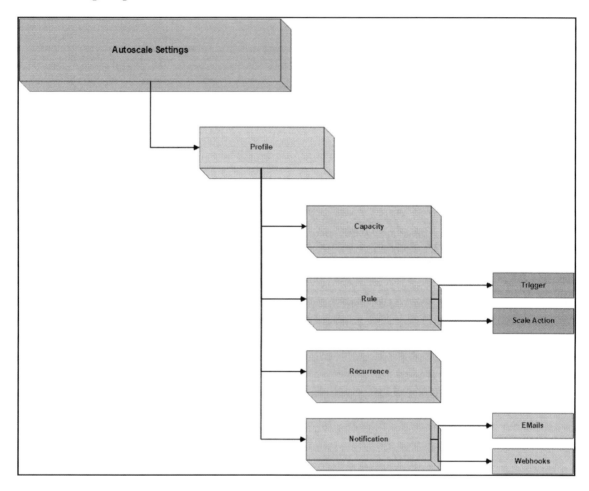

What is different here?

The profile shown contains an additional element called notifications. This element contains the following subelements:

- **Emails:** Emails are targets for the realization of alerts.
- **WebHook:** A WebHook can trigger multiple complex actions inside or outside of Azure. These actions include running **Azure Automation runbooks**, **Azure Functions**, **Azure Logic Apps**, or using third-party tools, such as **Twilio**.

Now let's come back to our question: what about vertical scaling?

The solution here is to use a WebHook, to run an Azure Automation runbook, which then performs the vertical scaling.

 Examples of such run books can be found here `https://gallery.` `technet.microsoft.com/scriptcenter/site/search`.

Where can I use autoscaling?

Currently, autoscaling is available as a build-in option for the following services:

- Azure Cloud Services
- Azure Service Fabric (scaling of SF clusters)
- Azure App Services (without Azure Functions)
- Azure VMs

Azure Functions (actually a part of Azure App Services) does not need the autoscaling build-in option because it scales automatically when needed. The autoscaling build-in option on Azure VMs is a special case because they only work in a so-called **VM Scale Set**.

A VM Scale Set can, by default, contain up to 100 identical VMs. But if you set the `singlePlacementGroup` property to `false` when you create the VM Scale Set, you can use up to 1,000 identical VMs.

With the help of autoscaling, you now have the option to automatically add VMs to your scale set until the limits are reached. The deployment takes place within a few minutes.

Summary

In this chapter, we've continued our insight into certain architectural aspects that are important in the daily use of the Azure platform and are part of the design process for your own Azure solutions. The topics of performance and scalability were the focus of our consideration. You've learned the basics and direct references to the Azure platform (for example, performance levels for Azure VMs).

In the next chapter, we will continue with our series on special architectural aspects, this time with a focus on the topics of monitoring and telemetry.

7
Monitoring and Telemetry

In the last two chapters, I've tried to extend our current perspective on Azure to specific architectural aspects. These aspects affect our day-to-day work and therefore, the design process for our own Azure solutions.

So far, the focus has been on availability, performance, and scalability. All three themes have one thing in common. They only work with telemetry data and sophisticated monitoring solutions.

In order to fully deal with the topic, we will focus on monitoring and telemetry in this chapter.

This chapter is divided into two parts. In part one, we discuss the question of what type of data we are actually talking about. Then, in part two, I will introduce you to the possible solutions for capturing this data.

We will explore the following topics in detail in this chapter:

- Telemetry data
- An overview of monitoring
- Azure management portal
- System specific tools
- Microsoft System Center
- Microsoft **Operations Management Suite (OMS)**
- Azure Monitor
- Azure Application Insights
- Grafana
- Azure Log Analytics
- Azure Network Watcher

About telemetry data

Let's start with the question: What is telemetry data? The term **telemetry**, refers to the transmission of measured values from a sensor to a spatially separated location.

At this receiving point, the measured values are either only recorded and collected, or transferred directly to an evaluation process.

The acquisition of telemetry data is often supplemented by a path of action to the detecting sensor, so as to be able to respond to the delivered measured values with suitable actions. This return path is called **remote control**.

Let's move on to the area of **monitoring**. Here, we could also talk about a telemetry process. For example, a network device can assume the role of a sensor and constantly transmit data about the state of the connection, latency, and much more.

Although we can speak of telemetry, I would like to introduce a second term that is more common when using monitoring solutions: **metrics**.

What is a metric?

A metric is a collection of telemetry data that is visualized within the monitoring solution and provided in a monitoring dashboard.

In the area of metrics, we know two types and, according to the level of abstraction, five classifications.

Types of metrics are:

- Pre-defined or common metrics
- Custom metrics

What is the difference between these two types? While common metrics come in the context of general infrastructure elements (for example, to measure the CPU usage), custom metrics cover all user-defined measurement points.

Classifications of metrics are:

- **Client metrics**: Client metrics are concerned with measuring the perception of the end user, for example, how long does it take for a client application to process and render results? Other areas covered by client metrics are the responsiveness of local and remote operations, the memory footprint, and the CPU usage.

- **Business metrics**: Business metrics provide a viewpoint to the logical operations (all end user activities) that define the business process. In terms of best practice, business metrics should cover all business transactions that the system performs.
- **Application metrics**: Application metrics include all measurements of the activity and performance of the application layer (that is, the application code, all application frameworks, and runtime execution environments used by the application). The purpose of these metrics is to help you synchronize the flow through the application with a potentially large number of concurrent user requests, analyze the resources that are consumed, and evaluate the likelihood and causes of performance issues.
- **System metrics**: System metrics capture information about the performance of the underlying infrastructure. These metrics are typically focused on **Key Performance Indicators** (**KPIs**) associated with memory occupancy, network utilization, disk activity, and CPU use.
- **Service metrics**: Service metrics cover the performance of dependent services, such as Azure Storage, messaging, cache, database, and any other external services your application may use. However, these types of metrics do not measure the performance of these services themselves, but capture information about the performance of the queries your system sends to them.

Let's look again at the classifications in detail.

Client metrics

Let's start with the general definition: **client metrics** give you an insight into the use of the system by an end user. All metrics at this level typically depend on how responsive the UI is, and how many client-side resources the application consumes.

Many modern user interfaces are browser or device based. In these situations, the primary measured values are those that are related to page views, page load time, JavaScript code, the browser or device types' geographical location, and session traces.

How do I collect the data from client metrics?

The common solution is to include JavaScript code in client-side code that records the necessary information. This code can then capture metrics such as page load times, session data (the life cycle of an interaction that can span multiple web pages and operations), JavaScript and other client-side code exceptions, or AJAX time information.

The JavaScript code sends this data to a service that collects and retrieves and inspects this information.

Azure Application Insights follows this approach. All you have to do is to manually include calls to Application Insight API functions in the code of your Azure solution.

 In order to make it as easy as possible to integrate the API calls, Microsoft offers you various Application Insight SDKs for various programming languages. All SDKs are open source projects and accessible via the following home page: `https://github.com/Microsoft/ApplicationInsights-Home`.

What data is collected?

The most frequently collected data includes:

- Page views
- Page load times
- Time spent visiting a page
- Session traces
- Client-side environment statistics
- JavaScript and HTML rendering errors
- The geographic location of clients
- Session ID and user ID for each request

While most of these metrics are single values only, the session traces and the client-side environment statistics metrics collect entire collections of data.

Every session trace includes a timeline with entries for all operations included in a session, and all resources used by this session.

These entries include:

- Information about each loaded asset
- Information about each AJAX request
- Logs for all user interactions (such as clicks and scrolls)
- Logs for all JavaScript events
- Logs for every exception

The client-side environment statistics situation is a bit more complicated. The client-side code can be run on a variety of different devices and operating systems, such as different versions of Windows, Android, and iOS, as well as accessing a wide selection of browsers, such as Microsoft Edge, Internet Explorer, or Safari.

You must therefore, at any time, get information about devices, operating systems and selected browser capture, and in any combination.

Business metrics

Let's start again with the general definition: **business metrics** are about measuring and assessing business operations and transactions. You can use this information to determine if your application meets the previously-set business expectations.

An example: your application is a video streaming service. Typical business metrics for this would be:

- A measure of the number of videos uploaded or downloaded over a period of time
- A measure of the frequency at which videos are searched
- A measure of how often videos have been watched successfully

Let's go back to the definition and go deeper into the details: a **business metric** typically includes telemetry inspection and aggregation at the enterprise level, as well as real-time snapshots and system behavior histories. This is then combined with a deeper study of pivots, time slices, and property filters, resulting in an accurate assessment of the business impact on the system.

In addition to creating this analytical data, business metrics also address more immediate issues, such as determining why business operations may fail, and alerting when different performance thresholds are exceeded.

How do I collect the data from business metrics?

Most **Application Performance Management** (**APM**) tools are designed to collect this kind of information. But they do not use general metrics and instead, rely on the results of so-called **profiler runs**.

What is a profiler?

A **profiler** is an agent (an application) that encapsulates a profiling API (such as the .NET profiling API). This agent then registers in the runtime environment (for example, the CLR) as a profiler, when running the application.

The runtime environment then calls the agent when code is loaded, and the agent orchestrates the code using a byte-code injection. This process is transparent to your application and does not require any modification of your code in any way.

In case you want to gather additional information, some APM tools provide APIs that can be used to capture and store data for custom metrics. However, this requires a change in the code of your applications.

On the Azure platform, business metrics will be using Azure Application Insights and New Relic's third-party solution (New Relic APM).

What data is collected?

The most frequently collected data includes:

- Business transactions that violate a performance goal (**service level objective (SLOs)**)
- Business transactions that fail
- Throughput and response time of business transactions

Application metrics

Let's start again with the general definition: an **application metric** provides you with an insight on a lower level. You get answers to questions such as: How well does the application handle the workload? What happens in the application under the hood and why?

To gather this information, you must track application logic, monitor database connection requests, and all the application's calls to store and retrieve data. Furthermore, you should also cover the use of dependent services by the application (for example cache, service bus, authorization/authentication, and so on). For a complete picture, you should also collect application framework metrics such as ASP.NET performance counters or CLR performance counters (only .NET framework), details about exceptions triggered by the application, details about application locks, and used threads.

How do I collect the data from application metrics?

Most of the application metrics can be easily captured using the system-level performance counters or other functions provided by the operating system.

Also, the instrumentation of many **Application Performance Management** (**APM**) tools (such as Azure Application Insights) can be configured to collect data without having to manually change the code. Instead, checkpoints are inserted that can capture all the information generated when a transaction starts and completes, or is generated by additional services (such as databases, storage, authentication, and authorization, or third-party web APIs).

Not enough? Alternatively, you can use your APM tool in combination with an application-logging framework (such as ILogger) or an extension API.

However, note that in this approach, you must manually add probes to your code that provide the information in the format expected by the APM.

What data is collected?

The most frequently collected data includes:

- Causes of high latency and low throughput
- Correlations between occurring exceptions and the activity performed
- Performance of the underlying application frameworks
- How much headroom is available in the system; (this means how far can your workload expand without exceeding the performance limits of the system?)

System metrics

Let's start again with the general definition: with system metrics, you can determine which system resources (for example, storage, network, CPU, and disk utilization) your system uses and where conflicts might occur.

You can use these metrics to see performance trends:

- As they grow linearly with time, you have to control the workload to see if it has increased and may need to be distributed to more hardware
- If the workload is constant, the increase in metrics' values may be due to external factors such as background tasks and jobs, additional network activity, or device I/O

How do I collect the data from system metrics?

You have two options for collecting system metrics:

- You can use Azure Diagnostics
- You can use PerfView

With Azure Diagnostics, you can collect diagnostic data for debugging and troubleshooting, measuring performance, monitoring resource usage, traffic analysis, capacity planning, and auditing.

With PerfView, you can collect and analyze performance data. PerfView enables you to perform investigations covering:

- CPU utilization
- Managed memory
- Unmanaged memory
- Timing and blockages

 PerfView was originally designed to run locally, but you can use `AzureRemotePerfView` (a NuGet package) to install and run PerfView remotely. You can find PerfView here: `https://www.microsoft.com/en-us/download/details.aspx?id=28567`. You can find `AzureRemotePerfView` here: `https://www.nuget.org/packages/AzureRemotePerfView`.

What data is collected?

The most frequently collected data includes:

- Physical memory utilization
- Managed memory utilization
- Network latency on the web server
- Network utilization on the web server
- Volume of network traffic
- Network overheads
- Network message payload size
- CPU utilization at the server and instance level
- CPU utilization on a specific server
- Processes exhibiting high levels of CPU utilization
- Excessive disk I/O

Service metrics

Let's start again with the general definition: most Azure applications and services depend on one or more other services (such as storage, caching, and messaging), and the performance of these dependent services can significantly affect how your system works. Therefore, it is important to monitor these elements, and service metrics are available for that.

How do I collect the data from service metrics?

The Azure portal provides service metrics for most Azure services (such as storage, SQL database, service bus, and so on). These metrics are often much more detailed than those provided through APM tools.

Dependent services can also provide their own application-level metrics. Examples for this include information on connection load, authentication exceptions for security services, process throttling during busy periods, and imminent restrictions due to approaching storage contingents. These metrics are useful for determining if the service is nearing capacity saturation and if it is currently available.

What data is collected?

The most frequently collected data includes:

- Azure Storage latency
- Volumes of traffic and throttling errors for Azure Storage
- Azure SQL Database connection failures
- Azure SQL Database DTU rates
- Excessive Azure SQL Database resource utilization
- Query performance
- Volumes of database requests
- Azure SQL Database deadlocks
- Service bus latency
- Service bus connection refusals and throttling
- Service bus failed requests and poison messages
- Event hub quota exceptions
- Event hub check-pointing failures and lease takeovers

An overview of monitoring

As I wrote earlier, in the second part of the chapter I would like to tell you about the different possible solutions and offerings for monitoring that the Azure platform provides.

Take a look at the following diagram:

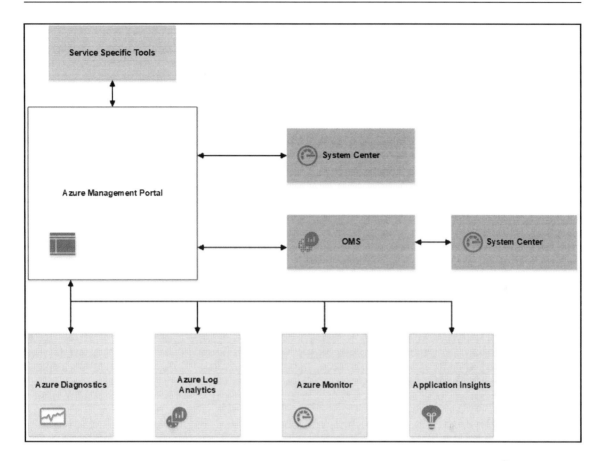

The key element in this overview is the Azure management portal. Each service offers its own monitoring capabilities via their respective dashboards.

Some services also have service-specific tools. This refers to tools that are installed locally but are nevertheless suitable for management and monitoring tasks in the cloud sector. The following are some examples:

- SQL Management Studio
- SQL Operations Studio
- Service Bus Explorer

Other tools that can be used to monitor your cloud are the Microsoft **System Center** (**SC**) and the Microsoft OMS. SC is a suite of tools for all conceivable management and monitoring tasks in the on-premises area. So, SC is meant primarily for your local IT, but can also be used in its functionality for the cloud.

OMS is a cloud-based solution that combines the management and the monitoring of your cloud environments, with the capabilities of the SC. The OMS can (or will) be used with an SC installation.

Finally, let's take a look at the monitoring solutions that the Azure platform itself has to offer. There are currently four of them:

- **Azure Diagnostics**: Azure Diagnostics is the classic offering and is used to collect diagnostic data for debugging and troubleshooting, measuring performance, monitoring resource usage, traffic analysis and capacity planning, and auditing. All data is stored in an Azure Storage account and is available for further processing. The only drawback is that Azure Diagnostics does not have its own surface for processing data. So, if you want to take advantage of the data, you have to organize your work manually.
- **Azure Log Analytics**: Azure Log Analytics is a tool that monitors your cloud-based, and also your local environments, to ensure their availability and performance. It collects data generated by resources in your cloud-based and local environments, as well as other monitoring tools, to enable analysis.
- **Azure Monitor**: Azure Monitor is a service, for monitoring and diagnosing Azure resources. However, you need to know that the Azure Monitor accesses existing (and therefore old) management capabilities of the Azure platform. These capabilities are, however, brought together for the first time in a common GUI, the Azure Monitor.
- **Azure Application Insights**: Azure Application Insights is an extensible for a developer-designed APM service that is available for multiple programming languages (for example, .NET, Java, or Node.js) and various platforms.

Azure management portal

The Azure portals provide dashboards that display specific metrics for Azure services that might not be available through APM tools or profilers. You can view, for example, the average latency of Azure Storage, or the rate for messaging within an Azure IoT Hub.

System specific tools

Some services (including third-party services) frequently provide their own monitoring and analysis utilities. Examples include the SQL Management views, and the **Query Performance** page in the SQL Management Studio.

These tools are dependent on the nature of the service being provided. For example, the **Query Performance** page in the SQL Management Studio lets you view the details of the query execution plan for recently executed SQL statements. If you have an understanding of how SQL Server optimizes queries, you might be able to use this information to make your queries more efficient.

Microsoft SC

SC is a suite of tools for all conceivable management and monitoring tasks in the on-premises area.

SC consists of the following components:

- System Center Configuration Manager
- System Center Data Protection Manager
- System Center Operations Manager
- System Center Orchestrator
- System Center Service Manager
- System Center Virtual Machine Manager
- System Center Service Management Automation
- System Center Service Provider Foundation

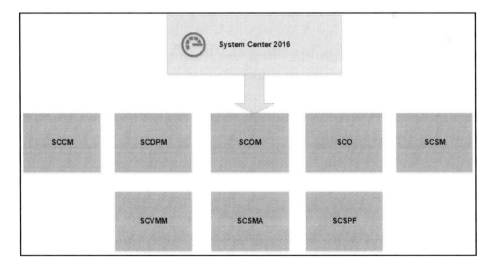

So, SC is meant primarily for your local IT, but can also be used in its functionality for the cloud. A special case are the components, System Center Orchestrator and System Center Service Management Automation, as there is already an equivalent cloud offering with Azure Automation.

Microsoft OMS

As we have already discussed the basics in `Chapter 4`, *Networking Design and Management*, let's get into detail. The OMS is a cloud-based solution that combines the management of your cloud environments, with the capabilities of the System Center (SC 2016).

It does not matter whether it is a private cloud, a public cloud, or a hybrid cloud, or whether it uses Microsoft Azure or a third-party cloud provider (for example, AWS or OpenStack). OMS also does not differentiate between Windows Server or Linux, or between virtualization based on Hyper-V or VMware.

The OMS is divided into the following areas:

- Insight and Analytics
- Automation and control
- Security and compliance
- Protection and recovery

Numerous individual tools and features are available for each of these areas. Because of the large number, I can't, unfortunately, go into it here. If you need further information, visit the **Solution Gallery** of your OMS Workspace.

Tip 1: If you visit the **Solution Gallery**, you should look at the OMS **Network Performance Monitor**.

Tip 2: Microsoft offers an integration add-in for your on-premises system center environment.

For comprehensive information about the OMS, you should download the following free eBook, *Inside the Microsoft Operations Management Suite (Version 2.0)*, 750 pages, 2017 from: `https://gallery.technet.microsoft.com/Inside-the-Operations-2928e342`.

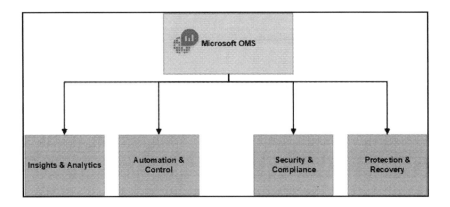

How do I start my work with the OMS?

If you have no experience with this suite, you should first choose a free OMS workspace (just register with a Microsoft account). You have to appreciate, though, that the amount of stored data is limited, as well as the period for which the data is kept.

Otherwise, you have two options for licensing. In option one shown here, you sign up to a subscription plan, which covers all components of the OMS and allows the use of the complete SC 2016:

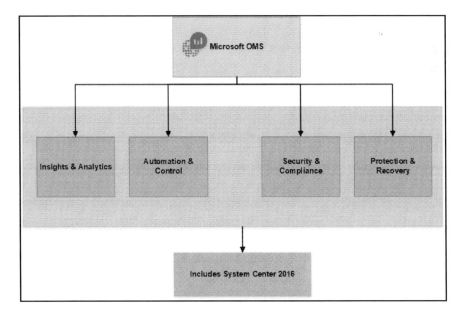

Alternatively, you can also license a single segment. Billing is then done via node (virtual machine, physical server, or network device). The license includes the use of the corresponding SC components.

In the following diagram, you can see the license model applied to the **Insights and Analytics** segment:

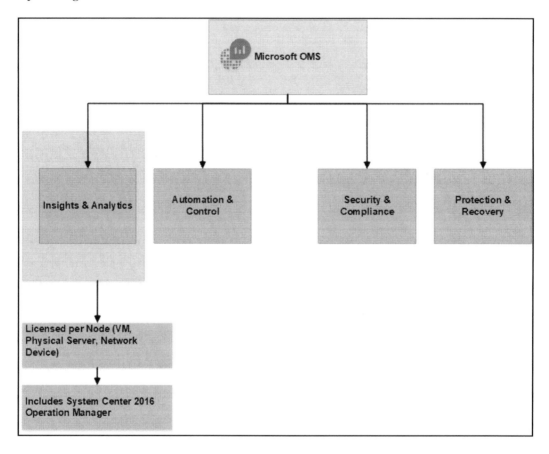

As you can see, licensing the **Insights and Analytics** section also includes usage rights to the SC 2016 **Operations Manager**.

For each of the OMS segments, numerous individual tools and features are available. Because of the large number, unfortunately, I cannot go into those further. So that you can get an idea of what they offer, however, we will take a closer look at the Insights and Analytics segment.

The Insights and Analytics segment includes the following capabilities:

- Activity log analytics
- Azure networking
- Service fabric analytics
- Active Directory replication status
- Alert management
- Wire data
- Container monitoring
- Surface hub monitoring (not really an Azure feature)
- DDI analytics
- Active Directory assessment
- Agent health
- Key vault monitoring
- Office 365 analytics
- SQL assessment
- VMware analytics

The segment also includes the following tools:

- Application Insights Connector
- Service Maps
- Network Performance Monitor

If you need more information about the other segments, just visit the **Solution Gallery** of your OMS workspace.

 For comprehensive information about the OMS, you should download the following free eBook: *Inside the Microsoft Operations Management Suite* (Version 2.0) 750 pages, 2017. Download from: `https://gallery.technet.microsoft.com/Inside-the-Operations-2928e342`.

Azure Monitor

As we have already discussed the basics in `Chapter 4`, *Networking Design and Management*, let's explore it in detail. Azure Monitor is an Azure service for monitoring and diagnosing Azure resources. However, you need to know that Azure Monitor generally accesses existing (and thus old) management capabilities of the Azure platform. These capabilities are, however, first brought together in a common GUI, the Azure Monitor.

Let's look at the work in detail:

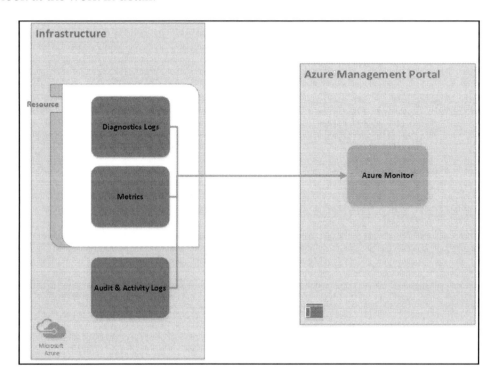

The preceding diagram shows the workflow as it is valid for general Azure resources (all Azure resources outside the compute area). The data for the monitoring is recorded at this workflow, on the infrastructure or the resource level.

Data sources at the infrastructure level are:

- **Audit and/or Activity Logs**: These logs contain all of the information about your Azure resource, from an infrastructure perspective. This information includes, for example, the creation or deletion time of resources.

Data sources at the resource level are:

- **Diagnostics Logs**: These protocols correspond to the output, the (standard) Azure diagnostics module of the various Azure services.
- **Metrics**: Available metrics vary by resource type. A VM represents, for example, a statistic on the CPU utilization in percentage ready. This value is not available for a service bus queue, but metrics such as queue size or throughput are available.

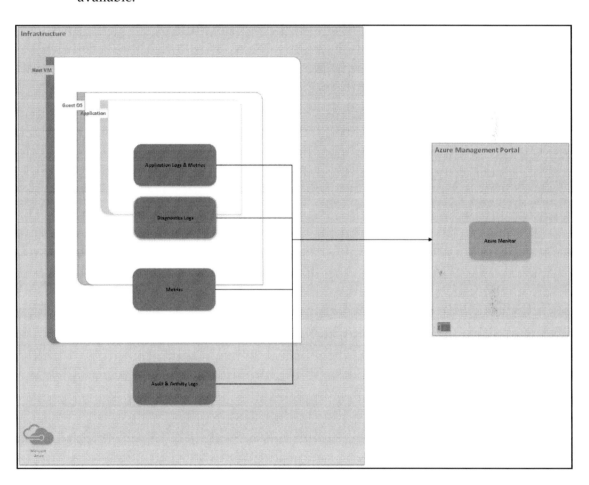

In the preceding diagram, it becomes somewhat more complicated. This shows the workflow as it is valid for compute Azure resources. The data for the monitoring is recorded at this workflow, on the infrastructure, the application, or the **Guest OS** level. Data at the **Host VM** level is currently not available.

Data sources at the infrastructure level are:

- **Audit and/or Activity Logs**: These logs contain all the information about your Azure resource, from an infrastructure perspective. This information includes, for example, the creation or deletion time of resources.

Data sources at the application level are:

- **Application Logs and Metrics**: It includes the following:
  - Counters
  - Application protocols
  - Windows event logs
  - .NET event source
  - IIS logs
  - Manifest-based ETW
  - Dump files
  - Error logs for customer applications
- **Diagnostics Logs**: These protocols correspond to the output, the (standard) Azure diagnostics module of the various Azure services

Data sources at the **Guest OS** level are:

- **Diagnostics Logs**: These protocols correspond to the output, the (standard) Azure diagnostics module of the various Azure services

Data sources at the host VM level are:

- **Metrics**: The available metrics vary depending on the resource type. However, because the host VM is an Azure VM, only metrics developed for VMs are available here.

Let's move on to the next diagram. Having seen the data sources for the Azure Monitor in the first two diagram, we can now focus on the main capabilities of the service:

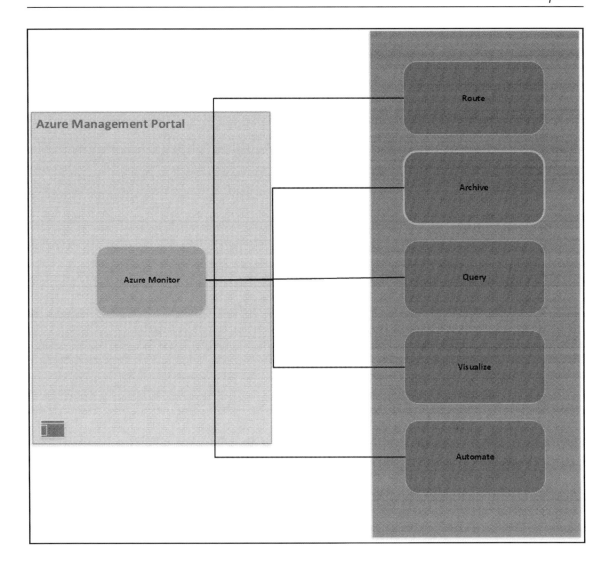

Which capabilities can be seen here?

The Azure Monitor has the following capabilities:

- **Route**: You have the opportunity to stream your monitoring data to other services or locations (for example, to Azure Event Hub or to Azure Application Insights). Among other things, this enables you to implement notification services for alarms or to process data in other environments.

- **Archive**: Monitoring data in the Azure Monitor is stored and available for a specified period of time (metrics for 30 days, activity log entries for 90 days). In addition, you have the option to forward monitoring data to an Azure Storage account for longer-term archiving. This is, however, subject to a charge.
- **Query**: You have the possibility to retrieve data for your own custom monitoring application or a third-party application using the Azure Monitor REST API, Azure CLI, Azure PowerShell or Azure .NET SDK.
- **Visualize**: By visualizing your monitoring data in graphs and charts, you can make trends faster than looking at the data yourself. Common tools for visualization include Azure Application Insights, Microsoft PowerBI, and numerous third-party tools.
- **Automate**: You can use the monitoring data to trigger alerts, events, or even entire processes. The most popular example of this is Azure autoscaling.

Which data (metric) is available?

Unfortunately, I cannot really answer that question, as several hundred metrics are available. The following list shows in which areas metrics are available:

- Analysis services
- API management
- Automation
- Autoscale
- Batch
- Cache (Redis Cache)
- Classic compute (Azure VM)
- Cognitive services
- Compute (Azure VM)
- CosmosDB
- Data Lake Analytics
- Data Lake Store
- Database for MySQL
- Database for PostgreSQL
- Device Provisioning Service (Azure IoT)
- Event Hub
- ExpressRoute
- IoT Hub

- Logic apps
- Network – public IP addresses
- Network – load balancer
- Network – traffic manager
- Network – virtual network gateways
- SQL database
- Storage
- Web apps

Enough of the theory, let's just take a look at how it works.

Here is a brief demonstration:

1. Open your Azure management portal at `https://portal.azure.com`.
2. In the navigation area of the portal, click on **Monitor**.
3. This opens the **Monitor** dashboard, as shown in the following screenshot:

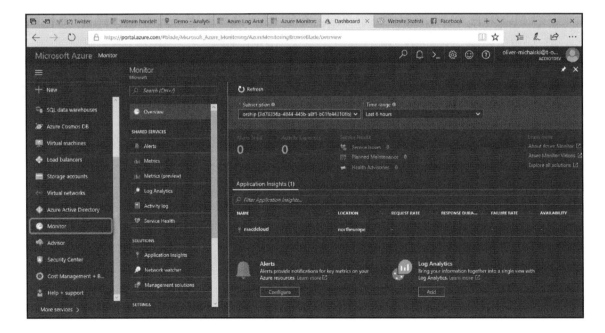

4. In the navigation area of the dashboard, click on **Metrics**.

5. This opens the metrics selection dialog.

6. The values for the **Subscription** selection field are preallocated, so you must first select a **Resource group** as shown in the following screenshot:

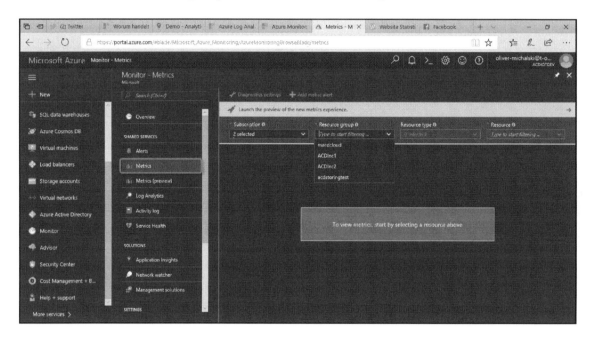

7. Next, you have to select a **Resource type** as shown in the following screenshot:

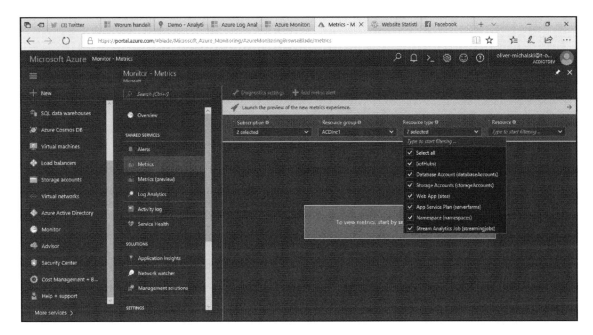

8. The last choice you have to make concerns the actual resource. Once you have made a selection, all the metrics available for the resource are displayed.

9. Select a metric and you will immediately see the corresponding chart.
10. As the last step, click on the **Pin** button as shown in the following screenshot:

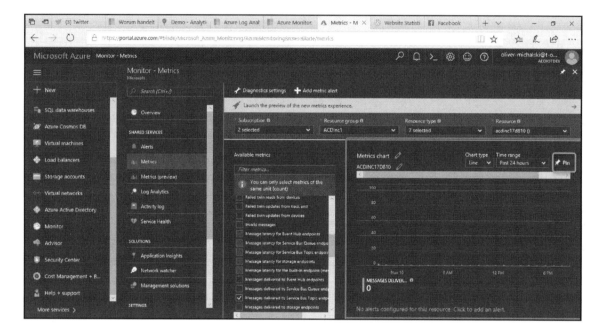

11. Now you get the **Metric chart** displayed on the default dashboard of the Azure management portal as shown in the following screenshot:

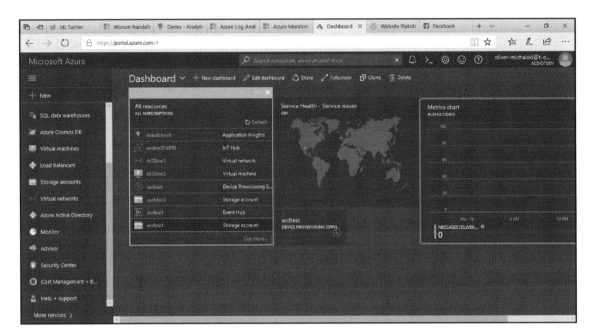

12. The metrics feature only gives you the ability to display values from a single metric. For the DevOps area, charts would be more interesting, that show several metrics in comparison at the same time. But with the multiple metrics charts, a new preview has recently been available. Let's take a look at this. In the navigation area of the dashboard, click on **Metrics (preview)**.

13. This opens the multiple metrics charts editor window. Here you first select a resource.

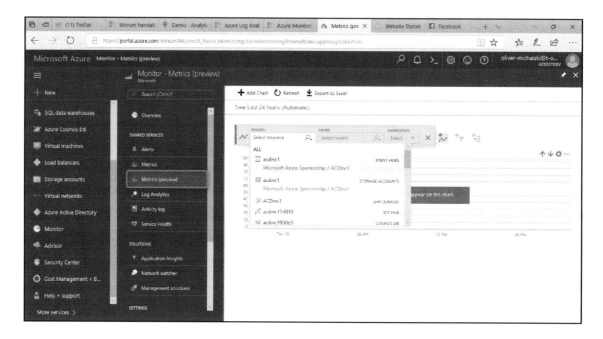

14. Selection of a **METRIC**:

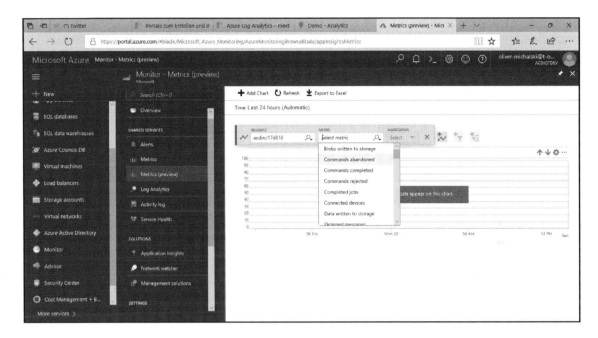

15. You can also determine what type of math value you want to see (for example, **Avg, Min, Max**) as shown in the following screenshot:

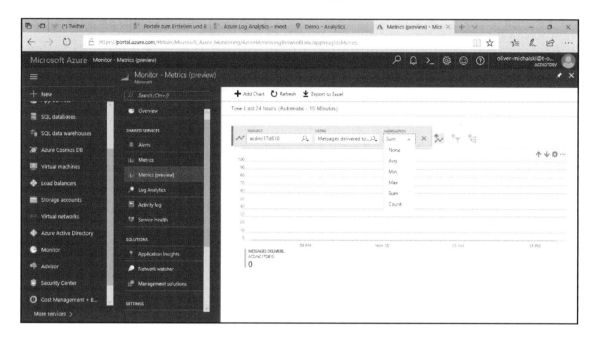

16. Now we've set the data picker for the first metric. Now click on the highlighted icon, and the selection procedure for the second metric starts. You can repeat this as often as you like.

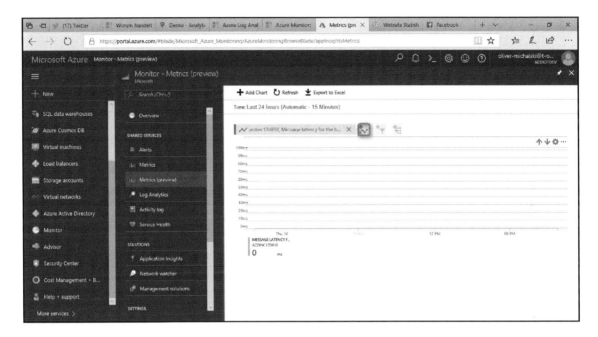

Azure Application Insights

Azure Application Insights is extensible for a developer-designed APM service that is available for multiple programming languages (for example, .NET, Java, or Node.js) and various platforms.

Azure Application Insights is the only service that is subject to constant change. Several times a year, there are updates to the service, and so it is virtually impossible to provide a complete description of the service.

But that should not stop me from providing you with at least a little overview to give you a better idea of Azure Application Insights.

Let's start with a simple question.

What data is captured by Azure Application Insights?

The following list is a compilation of the most frequently collected values:

- Request rates
- Response times
- Error rates
- AJAX calls on web pages (rating, response times, and error rates)
- Exceptions (server and browser exceptions)
- Page views
- Load balancing
- Number of users
- Number of sessions
- Performance counters from your Windows or Linux server (for example, CPU, memory or network usage)
- Host diagnostics for Azure and/or Docker environments
- Diagnostic trace logs
- Custom events or custom metrics (that is, client or server code you write yourself to track business events)

Enough of the theory, let's just take a look at how it works.

Here is a brief demonstration:

1. Open your Azure management portal at `https://portal.azure.com`.
2. In the navigation area of the portal, click on **Monitor**.
3. This opens the **Monitor** dashboard. In the navigation area of the dashboard, click on **Application Insights**.
4. Now, a list of existing Application Insights deployments opens. Find one and click in the **Name** field of the corresponding row.

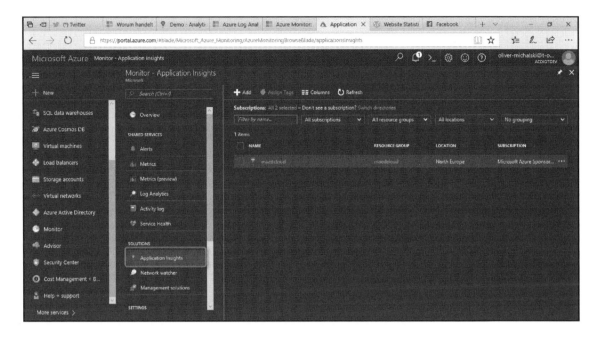

5. The corresponding dashboard of the deployment opens:

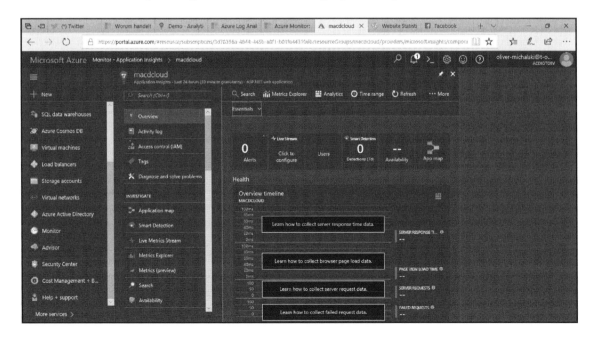

6. Now let's take a look at the selected Application Insights deployment in detail (as a diagram). Click on the **Application map** button in the navigation area of the dashboard and the diagram opens immediately:

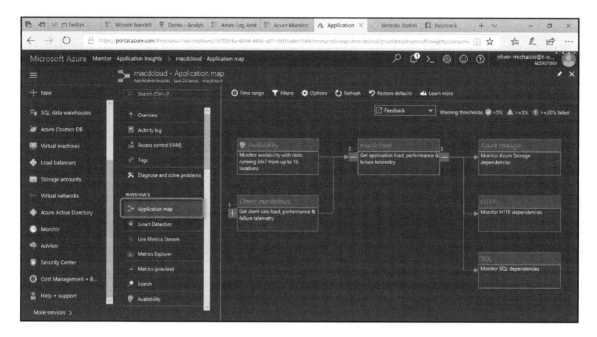

7. Do you want to examine your data instead? Click on the **Metrics Explorer** button in the navigation area of the dashboard and you can see your metrics charts:

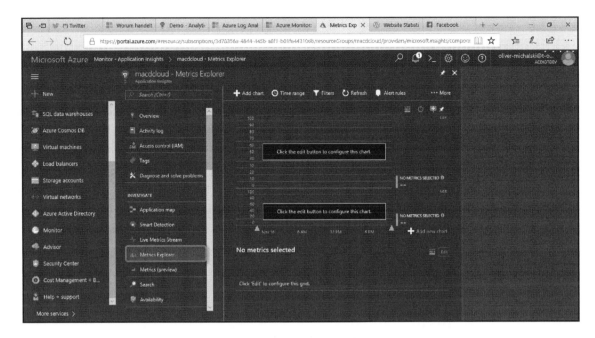

8. In addition to the **Metrics Explorer**, there are two other options for displaying data. The first is **Live Metrics Stream** and provides a display in real time:

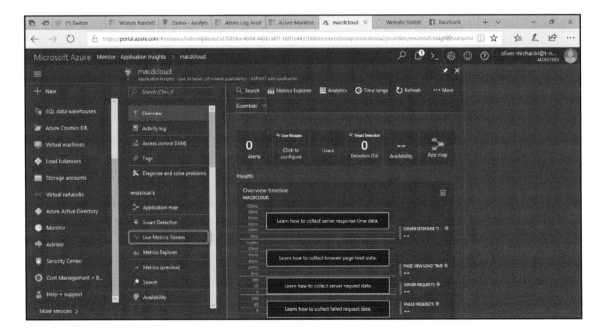

9. The second is **Metrics (preview)** and combines with the multiple metrics chart from Azure Monitor:

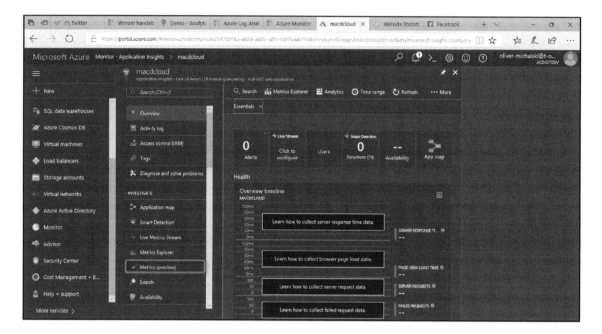

10. You want to analyze your data in-depth. Click the **Analytics** button in the top navigation bar of the dashboard:

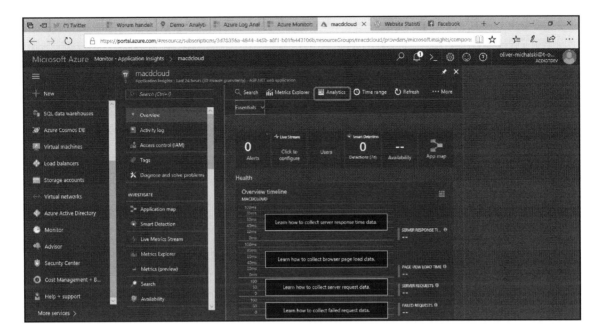

11. This opens the advanced **Analytics** portal for Azure Application Insights:

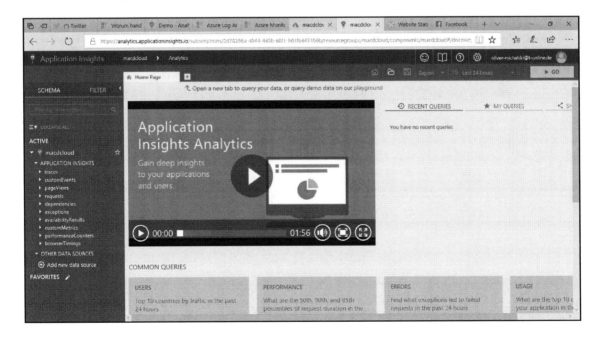

As I have already written, this is only a small overview. If you are looking for current information, it can be found here: `https://azure.microsoft.com/en-us/blog/tag/application-insights/`.

Grafana

In the previous two sections of this chapter, I introduced you to Azure Monitor service and Azure Application Insights. Now I would like to introduce you to a valuable extension that has been available for both services for a short time that is **Grafana**.

Grafana is an open source, feature-rich metrics dashboard and graph editor for more than 30 data sources (including Azure Monitor and Azure Application Insights).

With Grafana, you can query, visualize, or simply view your metrics, no matter where they are stored. You can create, explore, and share dashboards with your team.

How do I start my work with Grafana?

Grafana is hosted in the so-called **GrafanaCloud** offering you have the opportunity to register for a free account (single user) or a book a paid offering (from $ 19 per month).

You also have the option of setting up your own Grafana server (for example as Azure VM). A corresponding offering can be found in the Azure Marketplace.

Since Grafana is an open source project, you only pay for the pure Azure VM when bidding on the Azure Marketplace.
Resources:

- Grafana labs: `https://grafana.com/`.
- Grafana labs: GitHub: `https://github.com/grafana`.
- Azure Marketplace: `https://azuremarketplace.microsoft.com/en-us/marketplace/apps/grafana-labs.grafana_oss`.

Azure Log Analytics

Azure Log Analytics is a part of the OMS that monitors your cloud-based and, also your local environments, to ensure their availability and performance. It collects data generated by resources in your cloud-based and local environments, as well as other monitoring tools, to enable analysis.

If Azure Log Analytics is part of OMS, why do I need to talk about it again?

One of the key features of Azure Log Analytics is the ability to find data from multiple sources and aggregate it for analysis (Azure Log Analytics search).

This feature is exactly the reason we want to talk about Azure Log Analytics again. Since October 2017, Microsoft has been working on Azure Log Analytics version 2.0. The main innovation is a new (or at least heavily revised) Azure Log Analytics query language.

The most important innovations of the language are:

- **Simple and natural**: The new language is easier to understand and is similar to SQL. All constructs are in contrast to the previous query language rather than a natural language.
- **Piping functions**: The new language offers extensive piping functions. Almost every issue can be piped to another command. This allows complex queries to be created. That was not possible until now.
- **Field extractions at runtime**: The new language supports comprehensive fields calculated at runtime. You can perform complex calculations on extended fields, and then compute the computed fields for other commands, such as joins.
- **Extended joins**: The new language provides advanced joins, including the ability to join tables in multiple fields, use inner and outer joins, and join advanced fields.
- **Date and time functions**: The new language offers advanced date and time functions.
- **Intelligent analyses**: The new language uses advanced algorithms to evaluate patterns in datasets and compare different datasets.

Enough of the theory, let's just take a look at it.

Here is a brief demonstration:

1. Open your Azure management portal at `https://portal.azure.com`
2. In the navigation area of the portal, click on **Monitor**
3. This opens the **Monitor** dashboard. In the navigation area of the dashboard, click on **Log Analytics**:

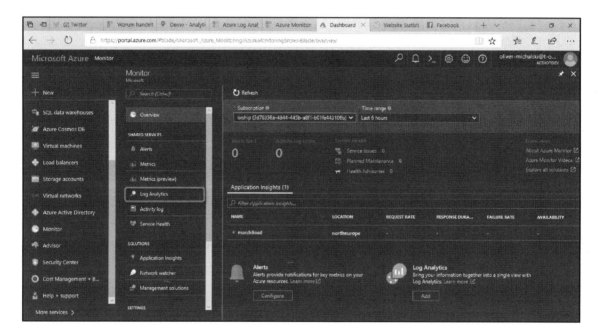

4. This opens the old **Log Search** editor page:

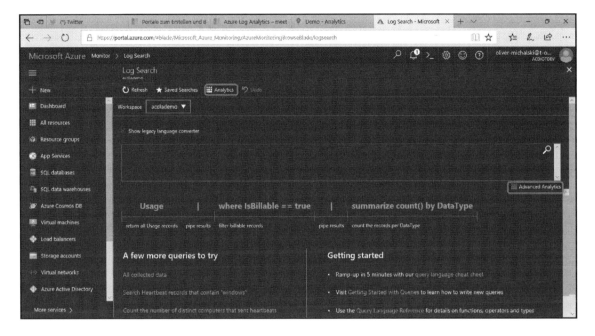

5. For the new features, click on **Analytics** or **Advanced Analytics**
6. The advanced **Analytics** portal opens. Note that this is the same portal used by Azure Application Insights.

The advanced **Analytics** portal provides new analytics capabilities that were not available on the old **Log Analytics** portal, such as multi-row editing in queries, additional visualizations, and advanced diagnostics.

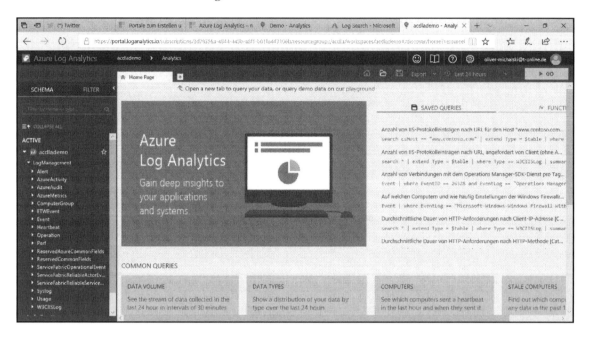

If you only want to learn about the elements of the Log Analytics query language and the features of the new workspace, you will find a complex demo here: `https://portal.loganalytics.io/demo#/discover/`.

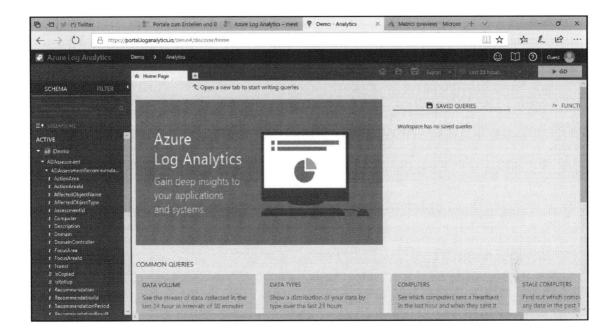

Azure Network Watcher

As we have already discussed the basics in Chapter 4, *Networking Design and Management*, let's explore it in detail. While the Microsoft OMS and the Azure Monitor are more general tools for management and monitoring, the tool I'm going to present is specifically designed for Azure networking is the Azure Network Watcher.

The Azure Network Watcher is a service that allows you to monitor and diagnose conditions at the level of network scenarios in Azure. The included tools for network diagnostics and visualization help you understand your network in Azure, perform diagnostics, and gain insights.

Currently, the Azure Network Watcher has the following features:

- **Topology**: Visualize your network topology
- **Network diagnostics**: Diagnostic tools for networking related issues:
    - Variable packet capture
    - IP flow verify
    - Security group view
    - Next hop
    - VPN troubleshooting
    - Connectivity check
- **Metric**: Measure and view of your network performance and health
    - Network subscription limits
- **Logs**: Configure and view your logs
    - Network security group flow logs

 One update: Since the Microsoft Ignite 2017 Conference (September 2017), the first preview of a Connectivity Check tool for Azure ExpressRoute is also available.

Summary

In this chapter, we've continued our insight into certain architectural aspects that are important to the daily use of the Azure platform, and are part of the design process for your own Azure solutions. The topic of monitoring and telemetry was the focus of our consideration. You've learned the basics of telemetry data and I've introduced you to the different solutions for capturing this data.

In the next chapter, we will continue with our series on special architecture aspects, this time with a focus on the topic of *Resiliency*.

8
Resiliency

In the previous chapter, you learned the basics of telemetry data in Azure and you explored the different solutions for capturing the data.

The focus of this new chapter will be on one more architectural aspect of an enterprise cloud-based solution—Resiliency.

The topics which we will cover in this chapter are as follows:

- Architecture design patterns for Resiliency
- Retry pattern with transient failures
- Load balancing
- Data replication
- Circuit Breaker pattern
- Throttling pattern
- Queue-Based Load Leveling pattern
- Compensating Transaction pattern

What is Resiliency?

On a cloud architecture (but in general on every IT system), you could have different events that could cause a failure of your solution. These failures could have a totally different nature, they could be hardware-related (a server goes down, a disk is corrupted and so on), they could be network-related (network glitches) or they could be data center-related (imagine a big problem on a data center or an Azure region).

When designing an architecture for the cloud, you need to have in mind that your solution could be affected by failures and you need to react to those failures, as soon as possible. This is the concept of Resiliency.

For a system, Resiliency (as a definition) is the ability to react to failures and continue to work. I've placed in evidence the word *react* because it's extremely important. You cannot totally avoid failures (some of them are totally unpredictable and not dependent on you), but you need to plan for a solution architecture that responds to failures in a quick way and permits you to guarantee as less downtime as possible, and no data loss.

Designing an application that is really resilient is not always so easy and it requires careful planning for and mitigating different types of failures that could occur. You need to identify possible failure points on your architecture and act as needed, in order to minimize them.

When planning for Resiliency of an architecture, there are three important metrics (business requirements) that you need to carefully evaluate:

- **Recovery time objective (RTO)**: The maximum acceptable time that an application can be unavailable after a failure
- **Recovery point objective (RPO)**: The maximum duration of data loss that is acceptable during a failure
- **Mean time to recover (MTTR)**: The average time needed to restore the application after a failure

A value for each of these metrics will determine a decision on how to plan your architecture. You need to carry out a careful failure analysis and plan for a solution that mitigates them. A useful checklist for Azure architectures is available here: `https://docs.microsoft.com/en-us/azure/architecture/resiliency/failure-mode-analysis`.

Resiliency can also be improved by carefully evaluating the **Service Level Agreement (SLA)** of each piece of your architecture (workloads).

For example, imagine having a business scenario where *n* remote applications send sales orders to a cloud-based web server (Azure VM) that collects them. Your business requirements dictate that your application must always be available for not missing orders that come from the remote sites.

In a first step, you can design the solution architecture like the following diagram:

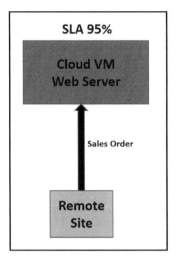

Here, the remote site sends a sales order directly to the central website (Azure VM), that, for example, could have an SLA of 95%. If the connection to the central website fails for some reason, the order transmittal is broken and the remote sites will be blocked on their transmissions. This could be a problem for your business scenario.

You could improve the Resiliency of your architecture by modifying the solution, like in the following diagram:

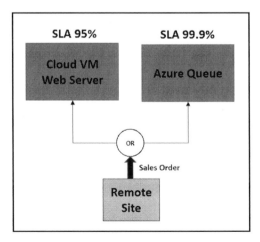

Here, the remote site sends an order to the remote web server (cloud VM). If the order transmission fails for some reason, the remote site will redirect the order transmission to an Azure Queue (that has a high level of SLA). Here, the order is queued (so no data loss) and it will be redirected to the central website when is available again. In this second scenario, you don't have data loss and you can guarantee an improved business continuity.

Architecture design patterns for Resiliency

There are common Resiliency strategies that are recommended that you check/implement when planning a resilient cloud architecture. The next sections will provide a brief summary of these different strategies and suggestions on how to implement these patterns in order to achieve Resiliency.

Retry pattern with transient failures

A transient failure is a common type of failure in a cloud-based architecture and often this is due to the nature of the network itself (loss of connectivity, timeout on requests, and so on).

A common way to react to these failures is to retry sending the request to the target application. You need to implement mechanisms that permit an automatic retry of requests if a failure occurs, maybe adding an increased delay between each retry attempt. This is commonly known as the **Retry pattern**.

In the Retry pattern, when there's a failure sending a request to a cloud service, the source application can react to this failure by providing the following actions:

- **Retry**: The source application can immediately retry to send the request to the cloud service. This is common when the failure event is classified as rare and the probability of a success when repeating the request is very high.
- **Retry after a delay**: The source application can retry to send the request to the cloud service after a period of time (that normally increases exponentially). This is a common practice when the failure event is due to reasons such as cloud service busy and so on.
- **Cancel**: The source application can cancel the request to the cloud service and throw (or log) the error. This is a common practice when the failure is not transient and there's a low probability that resending the request will be a success.

The following diagram shows a schema of the Retry pattern:

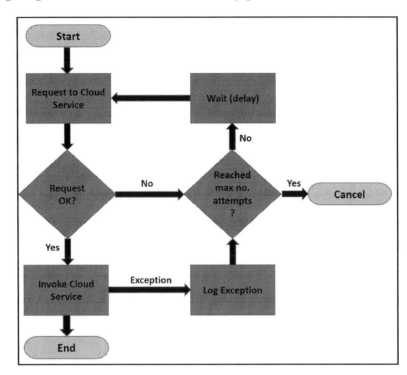

The Azure client SDK provides automatic retries by default for many different Azure services. For more information, you can check this official link on MSDN: `https://docs.microsoft.com/en-us/azure/architecture/best-practices/retry-service-specific`.

When implementing this pattern for your application, be careful to fine-tune the retry policy. A retry policy that is too frequent could impact on your application, making it become busy or unresponsive. A way to improve the reliability of this pattern could be to apply the Circuit Breaker pattern that we'll see in one of the following section.

As previously described, it's better to have an exponential backoff strategy for retry than a simple retry (fixed delay). With an exponential backoff strategy, the time between each retry is increased after each retry failure.

Always remember that this pattern is useful for handling transient faults, not for handling faults due to internal application exceptions (this should be done in a different way). Remember also that if your application receives too many faults due to the busy destination, this could be a sign that your cloud service must be scaled up.

An example of how you can implement a retry pattern in C# is as follows (console application):

```csharp
using System;
using System.Collections.Generic;
using System.Linq;
using System.Net.Http;
using System.Text;
using System.Threading.Tasks;

namespace RetryPattern
{
    class Program
    {
        static void Main(string[] args)
        {
            //Sending a request to a cloud service
            SendRequest();
        }
        static async void SendRequest()
        {
            HttpClient httpClient = new HttpClient();
            var maxRetryAttempts = 3;
            var pauseBetweenFailures = TimeSpan.FromSeconds(2);
            await
            RetryPattern.RetryOnExceptionAsync<HttpRequestException>
              (maxRetryAttempts, pauseBetweenFailures, async () =>
                {
                    var response = await httpClient.GetAsync(
                    "https://mycloudservice.com/api/items/1");
                    response.EnsureSuccessStatusCode();
                });
        }
    }
}
```

The `Main` function sends requests to a cloud service. If the request fails, the `RetryPattern` class handles the retry policy.

The class that implements the retry policy is as follows:

```csharp
public static class RetryPattern
    {
        public static async Task RetryOnExceptionAsync(
            int times, TimeSpan delay, Func<Task> operation)
        {
```

```
    await RetryOnExceptionAsync<Exception>(times, delay,
    operation);
}
public static async Task RetryOnExceptionAsync<TException>(
    int times, TimeSpan delay, Func<Task> operation) where
TException : Exception
{
    if (times <= 0)
        throw new ArgumentOutOfRangeException(nameof(times));
    var attempts = 0;
    do
    {
        try
        {
            attempts++;
            await operation();
            break;
        }
        catch (TException ex)
        {
            if (attempts == times)
                throw;
            await CreateDelayForException(times, attempts,
            delay, ex);
        }
    } while (true);
}
private static Task CreateDelayForException(
    int times, int attempts, TimeSpan delay, Exception ex)
{
    var _delay = IncreasingDelayInSeconds(attempts);
    return Task.Delay(delay);
}
internal static int[] DelayPerAttemptInSeconds =
{
    //Delay management for retry (exponential)
    (int) TimeSpan.FromSeconds(10).TotalSeconds,
    (int) TimeSpan.FromSeconds(40).TotalSeconds,
    (int) TimeSpan.FromMinutes(2).TotalSeconds,
    (int) TimeSpan.FromMinutes(10).TotalSeconds,
    (int) TimeSpan.FromMinutes(30).TotalSeconds
};
static int IncreasingDelayInSeconds(int failedAttempts)
{
    if (failedAttempts <= 0) throw new
    ArgumentOutOfRangeException();
    return failedAttempts > DelayPerAttemptInSeconds.Length ?
    DelayPerAttemptInSeconds.Last() :
```

```
                    DelayPerAttemptInSeconds[failedAttempts];
        }
    }
```

The `RetryPattern` class handles the retry of requests by counting the number of retries and using an exponential delay (wait time) before each retry.

 An interesting open source framework for implementing the Retry pattern (but also the Circuit Breaker pattern that we'll see in the next sections) is **Polly**. You can find more documentation here: `https://github.com/App-vNext/Polly`.

Load balancing

One of the ways to improve scalability and the Resiliency of a cloud application is to scale out the application itself by adding more instances when needed. This guarantees better performances in general and it can help to avoid busy services.

Load balancing is a common technique that allows for an improved distribution of workloads across multiple resources by optimizing the usage of a resource, its response time and its load.

With the Azure platform, if your service uses Azure App Service or Azure Cloud Services, they are already load balanced by the platform itself. However, if your application uses Azure Virtual Machines for your workloads, you will need to provision a load balancer.

With Azure, you can use Azure Load Balancer or Azure Traffic Manager to achieve this goal.

The difference between these two platforms are essentially:

- Azure Load Balancer routes traffic inside a region (round robin policy)
- Azure Load Balancer works at TCP/UDP level, routing traffic between endpoints that sits behind a public endpoint
- Azure Traffic Manager routes traffic globally based on flexible policies (not only round robin)
- Azure Traffic Manager works at DNS level, routing traffic between endpoints that sits behind a common DNS

When using VM for your workloads and you want to improve Resiliency, it's recommended you deploy the **virtual machines (VMs)** (at least two) in the same subnet and using the same availability set for the two VMs (this is a requirement for Azure Load Balancer). The Load Balancer will be configured to have a public IP address and clients will send the requests to the public IP address of the Load Balancer, which in turn will redirect the requests to the appropriate VM.

The following diagram shows the solution:

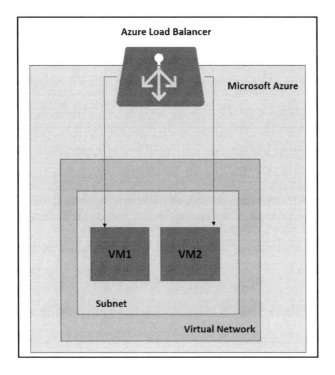

Now, imagine that you have two Azure VMs on the same subnet and on the same availability set, **myAvailSet** (they also have the same resource group called **MyRG**).

To create a Load Balancer in the Azure portal, perform the following steps:

1. Click on + and select **Networking** | **Load Balancer**:

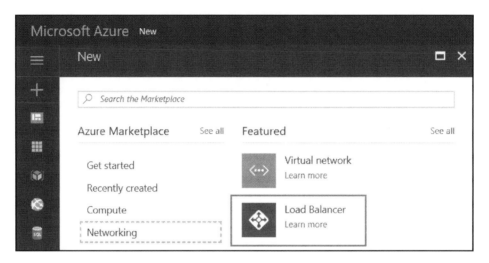

2. In the **Create load balancer** pane, give it a name of `PacktLoadBalancer`, select **Type** as **Public** and create a **Public IP address** by clicking on the appropriate section. Then select the Azure subscription to use and select **MyRG** as the **Resource group**:

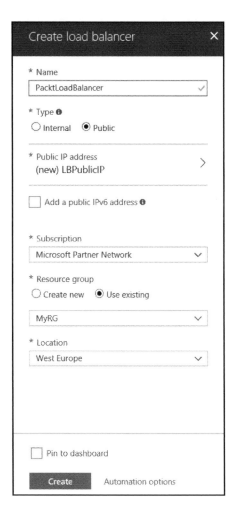

3. Click **Create** and the Load Balancer will be deployed.

4. When the Load Balancer is deployed, select it from your resources and select **Backend pools**:

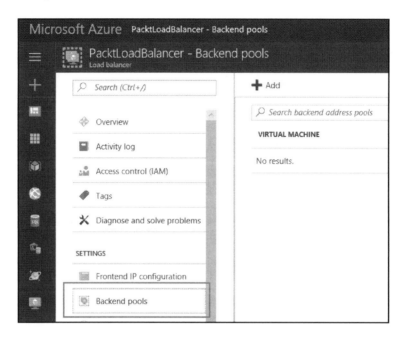

5. Click **Add** to create a new backend pool, give it a name, select **Associated to** as **Availability set** and select the **Availability set** of your Azure VMs as **myAvailSet**:

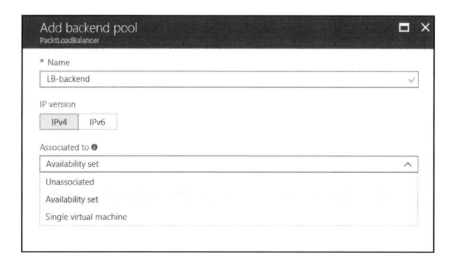

6. Now you can select the Azure VMs that you want to add under the Load Balancer:

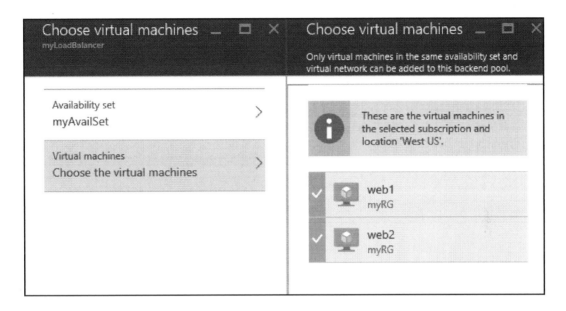

7. After adding the Azure VMs, you need to create what is called a health probe. Now click on **Health probes** | **Add** and configure your Load Balancer health probe here. Here, I've select **Protocol** as **HTTP** because my Load Balancer balances traffic on HTTP port 80:

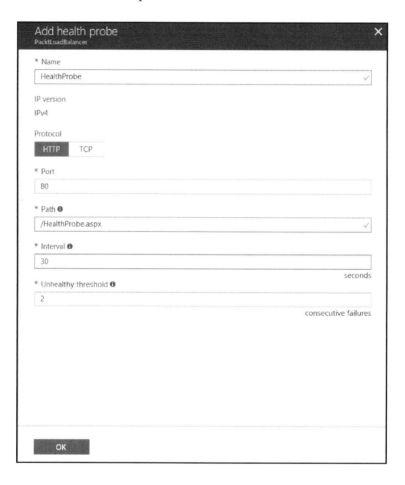

8. Click **OK** to deploy the health probe.
9. After the health probe creation, you need to create a Load Balancer rule by selecting the **Load balancing rules** option:

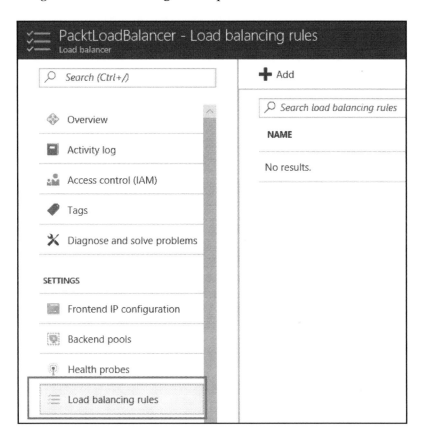

10. Click **Add** and create your load balancing rule:

11. The last step is creating your inbound NAT rules for forwarding the traffic from the Load Balancer to the VMs (inbound NAT rules forward traffic from frontend ports to backend ports). To do this, select the **Inbound NAT rules** option of the Load Balancer configuration, and create a new rule for every VM in your availability set:

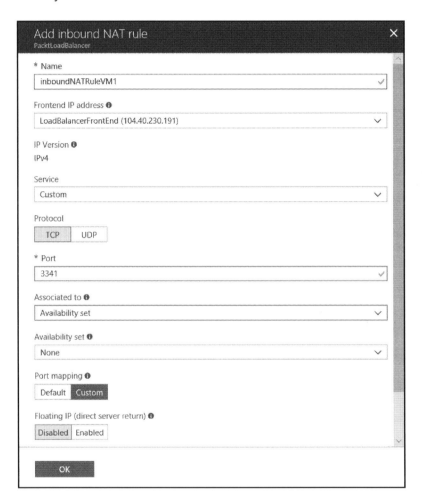

Your Load Balancing rule is now ready to go.

Data replication

When using cloud services for handling data, it's important to select the data replication strategy that best suits your business requirements. Azure Storage services have built-in replication. Replication copies your data, either within the same data center or to a second data center, depending on which replication option you choose.

The data in your Microsoft Azure storage account is always replicated to ensure durability and high availability. When you create a storage account, you have four replication options:

Replication option	Number of copies	Strategy
Locally redundant storage (LRS)	Maintains three copies of your data	Data is replicated three times within a single facility in a single region
Zone-redundant storage (ZRS)	Maintains three copies of your data	Data is replicated three times across two to three facilities, either within a single region or across two regions
Geo-redundant storage (GRS)	Maintains six copies of your data	Data is replicated three times within the primary region and is also replicated three times in a secondary region hundreds of miles away from the primary region
Read-access geo-redundant storage (RA-GRS) (default)	Maintains six copies of your data	Data is replicated to a secondary geographic location, and also provides read access to your data in the secondary location

 You can also change the replication option after the creation of your storage account unless you specified ZRS at the time of the account creation. You may have an additional one-time data transfer cost if you switch from LRS to GRS or RA-GRS.

From the Azure portal, when creating a storage account you can select the replication option that best suits your business needs:

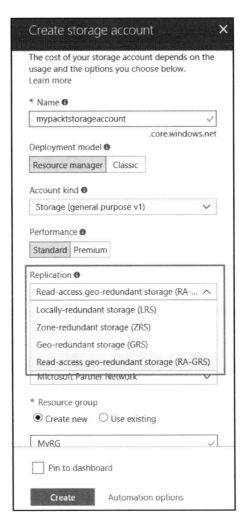

Data replication is an important aspect to consider on an Azure architecture. Carefully plan your data replication strategy according to the business needs.

Circuit Breaker pattern

In many scenarios, when a cloud service is down (or not responding), in order to achieve Resiliency you can prevent an application from continuously re-sending a request to the cloud service. This architectural behavior is achieved via the Circuit Breaker pattern. The state diagram of this pattern is represented in the following figure:

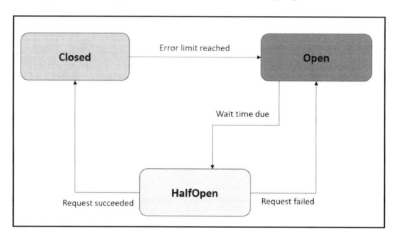

When application A sends requests to cloud service B, we're in the **Closed** state. In this state, if some error occurs the Circuit Breaker pattern counts these errors and when the predefined error limit is reached, the state becomes **Open**.

When we're in the **Open** state, requests from application A to cloud service B are stopped (the pattern could throw an exception or log the error).

After a certain amount of time (defined according to the business scenario), the state will switch to **HalfOpen**. In the **HalfOpen** state, the application can again send a request to cloud service B. If the request has a success, the state will become **Closed** and the communication between A and B will become healthy, otherwise, the state of the circuit is switched back to **Open**.

As you can see, this pattern prevents a situation where application A continuously sends requests that fail to cloud service B (down), resulting in an unstable system with a high load traffic (or CPU).

An important aspect to remember—the purpose of the Circuit Breaker pattern is different to the Retry pattern. The Retry pattern enables an application to retry an operation in the expectation that it'll succeed. The Circuit Breaker pattern prevents an application from performing an operation that is likely to fail.

To see an example of how to implement the Circuit Breaker pattern, consider an application that sends orders to a remote service (here it is a database) and reads the order status. The following lines of code show a C# console application (available on GitHub) that uses the Circuit Breaker pattern.

The order is represented by the `Order` object (C# class):

```
public class Order
    {
        public int ID { get; set; }
        public decimal Value { get; set; }
        public override string ToString()
        {
            return $"{{ Order ID: {ID}, Order Value: '{Value}'}}";
        }
    }
```

In the `Main` function, the console application instantiates the `CircuitBreakerRepository` class (pattern implementation) that connects to the remote service via the `ServiceConnectionFactory` class and randomly sends read or write requests to the remote service by calling the `ReadOrWrite` function:

```
class Program
    {
        static void Main(string[] args)
        {
            int requestToSend = 100;
            // Create a circuit breaker repository
            IOrderRepository repository = new
          CircuitBreakerRepository(ServiceConnectionFactory.Connection);
            for (int i = 0 ; i < requestToSend; i++)
            {
                try
                {
                    ReadOrWrite(repository, i);
                }
                catch (Exception e)
                {
                    Console.WriteLine($"{ex.GetType().FullName}:
                    {ex.Message}");
                }
                Thread.Sleep(1000);
            }
        }

        static void ReadOrWrite(IOrderRepository repository, int i)
```

```
        {
            var random = new Random();
            if (random.Next(50) > 25)
            {
                // make a write
                var order = new Order
                {
                    ID = i,
                    Value = 100 + i
                };
                repository.Write(order);
                Console.WriteLine($"Write Request: {order}");
                Console.WriteLine("");
            }
            else
            {
                // make a read
                Console.WriteLine($"Read Request: {string.Join(", ",
                repository.Read())}");
                Console.WriteLine("");
            }
        }
    }
```

The class `CircuitBreakerRepository` implements the interface `IOrderRepository`
(that contains the `Read` and `Write` methods for requests):

```
public interface IOrderRepository
    {
        List<Order> Read();
        void Write(Order order);
    }
```

The pattern is as follows:

```
public class CircuitBreakerRepository : IOrderRepository
    {
        private CircuitBreakerState _state;
        private OrderRepository _repository;

        public CircuitBreakerRepository(MongoClient client)
        {
            _state = new CircuitBreakerClosed(this);
            _repository = new OrderRepository(client);
        }

        public List<Order> Read()
        {
```

```
        return _state.HandleRead();
}

public void Write(Order order)
{
    _state.HandleWrite(order);
}
private abstract class CircuitBreakerState
{
    protected CircuitBreakerRepository _owner;
    public CircuitBreakerState(CircuitBreakerRepository owner)
    {
        _owner = owner;
    }
    public abstract List<Order> HandleRead();
    public abstract void HandleWrite(Order order);
}

private class CircuitBreakerClosed : CircuitBreakerState
{
    private int _errorCount = 0;
    public CircuitBreakerClosed(CircuitBreakerRepository owner)
        :base(owner){}
    public override List<Order> HandleRead()
    {
        try
        {
            return _owner._repository.Read();
        }
        catch (Exception e)
        {
            _trackErrors(e);
            throw e;
        }
    }

    public override void HandleWrite(Order order)
    {
        try
        {
            _owner._repository.Write(order);
        }
        catch (Exception e)
        {
            _trackErrors(e);
            throw e;
        }
    }
```

```
        private void _trackErrors(Exception e)
        {
            _errorCount += 1;
            if (_errorCount > Config.CircuitClosedErrorLimit)
            //Limit of error requests to accept
            {
                _owner._state = new CircuitBreakerOpen(_owner);
            }
        }
    }
    private class CircuitBreakerOpen : CircuitBreakerState
    {
        public CircuitBreakerOpen(CircuitBreakerRepository owner)
            :base(owner)
        {
            new Timer( _ =>
            {
                owner._state = new CircuitBreakerHalfOpen(owner);
            }, null, Config.CircuitOpenTimeout, Timeout.Infinite);
        }

        public override List<Order> HandleRead()
        {
            throw new CircuitOpenException();
        }
        public override void HandleWrite(Order order)
        {
            throw new CircuitOpenException();
        }
    }
    private class CircuitBreakerHalfOpen : CircuitBreakerState
    {
        private static readonly string Message = "Call failed when
        circuit half open";
        public CircuitBreakerHalfOpen(CircuitBreakerRepository
        owner)
            :base(owner){}

        public override List<Order> HandleRead()
        {
            try
            {
                var result = _owner._repository.Read();
                _owner._state = new CircuitBreakerClosed(_owner);
                return result;
            }
            catch (Exception e)
            {
```

```
                _owner._state = new CircuitBreakerOpen(_owner);
                throw new CircuitOpenException(Message, e);
            }
        }
        public override void HandleWrite(Order order)
        {
            try
            {
                _owner._repository.Write(order);
                _owner._state = new CircuitBreakerClosed(_owner);
            }
            catch (Exception e)
            {
                _owner._state = new CircuitBreakerOpen(_owner);
                throw new CircuitOpenException(Message, e);
            }
        }
    }
}
public static class Config
{
    public static int CircuitOpenTimeout => 5000;
    public static int CircuitClosedErrorLimit = 10;
}
```

In the `Main` function, the application sends *n* requests to the remote service (read or write requests are randomly selected). When the remote service is down, the application receives an exception from the remote host until the accepted error limit is reached (check the `_trackErrors` function).

When this limit is reached (in the preceding example there are 10 error requests), the machine state goes into the opened state. All requests to the remote service are now stopped and the retry will succeed after the `CircuitOpenTimeout` elapsed time.

Throttling pattern

A typical cloud application can have a variable load over time based on different situations such as a number of concurrent requests, a number of active users over time, types of actions that the application must perform and so on. In each of these situations, resources could become insufficient and the application could have poor performances or it could have a failure.

One common way to handle these situations is to scale the application accordingly by adding more instances, but as you can imagine this approach has two main side-effects—costs and time to scale up a new instance.

The Throttling pattern is an approach that permits a cloud application to use resources up to a defined limit. When the limit is exceeded, the client is throttled for a certain period of time and during this time, the cloud application blocks all requests from that client. The cloud application should return an exception to the client indicating the throttling reason.

A standard schema for the Throttling pattern is described in the following diagram:

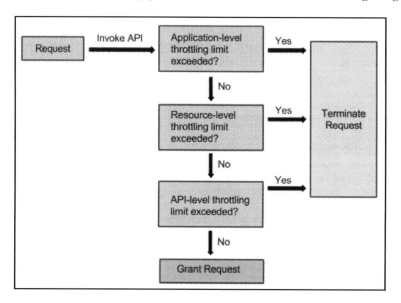

Azure Resource Manager (ARM) limits read requests to 15,000 per hour and write requests to 1,200 per hour for a single ARM instance, for each subscription and tenant. If the request limit is reached, your application receives an HTTP status code **429 too many requests** and a Retry-After value in the header. The Retry-After value specifies the number of seconds that your application should wait before sending a new request. If the application sends a request before the Retry-After value has elapsed, the request is not processed and ARM returns a new Retry-After value.

If in your business scenario, you have multiple concurrent applications that make requests on the same subscription, all the requests are added together to determine the number of remaining requests. Each response header of every request includes values for the number of remaining read and write requests.

For example, in C#, you can retrieve the remaining number of the subscription scoped reads by checking the header value from an `HttpWebResponse` object (here called `response`) with the following line of code:

```
response.Headers.GetValues("x-ms-ratelimit-remaining-subscription-
reads").GetValue(0)
```

These response headers values are listed in the following link: `https://docs.microsoft.com/en-us/azure/azure-resource-manager/resource-manager-request-limits`.

Queue-Based Load Leveling pattern

In many cloud scenarios, during a day, a service could have peaks of traffic (periods where the number of requests from sender applications is extremely high) and this could affect the performances of the entire architecture and of your business level.

To avoid these situations, a common architectural strategy is to use a queue that acts as a buffer of requests and permits you to decouple the sender from the receiver. Check this Microsoft diagram:

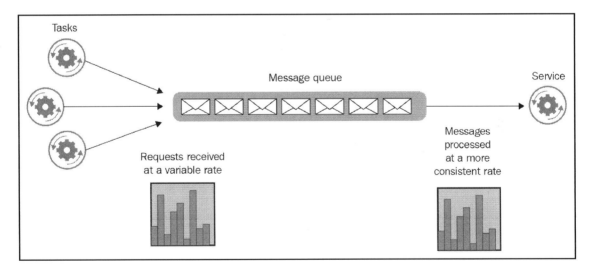

In this architecture, a sender, instead of directly sending a request to a cloud service, it sends a request to a message queue. Then, the cloud service retrieves the messages from the message queue and processes the request. What's important to note here is that the requests could arrive at the message queue with an extremely high volume, while the cloud service processes them at the desired rate. This ensures that the cloud service will never be busy or heavy load. The main advantages here are as follows:

- **Reliability and availability**: No messages are lost due to a failed request (timeout)
- **Scalability**: You can increase the number of queues or services according to your business needs

Regarding the Azure platform, we can have two types of queue mechanisms:

- **Azure Storage queues**: Simple REST-based interface for message exchange between services (GET, PUT, PEEK). They are part of the Azure storage infrastructure. A queue message can be up to 64 KB in size and the number of messages is limited to the storage account capacity. The **time-to-live (TTL)** of a message is 7 days.
- **Azure Service Bus**: A more advanced mechanism that supports queues, topics, relays and message size up to 256 KB. The TTL of a message in a Service Bus queue can be unlimited. For more information, visit `https://docs.microsoft.com/en-us/azure/service-bus-messaging/service-bus-fundamentals-hybrid-solutions`.

Here, we'll show you how to use Azure Service Bus to implement a queue-based pattern:

1. In Azure portal, click on + and select **Enterprise Integration** | **Service Bus**:

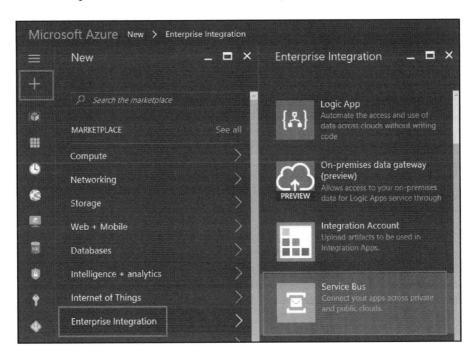

2. In the **Create namespace** pane, give the name of your Service Bus queue and select resource group and location:

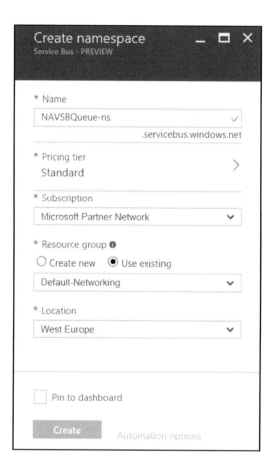

3. Now select the **Queues** option and add a new queue:

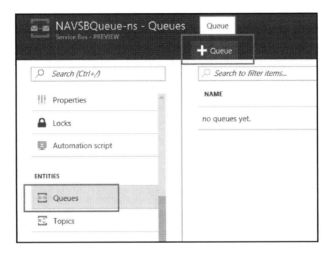

4. Select the queue name and set the queue parameters such as queue size and TTL:

5. Click **Create** and your Azure Service Bus queue will be provisioned and ready to be used (you can find the queue URL and the **Shared Access policies** option where you find the connection string):

6. When a client application sends a message to the queue, you can directly monitor the queue via the Azure portal itself:

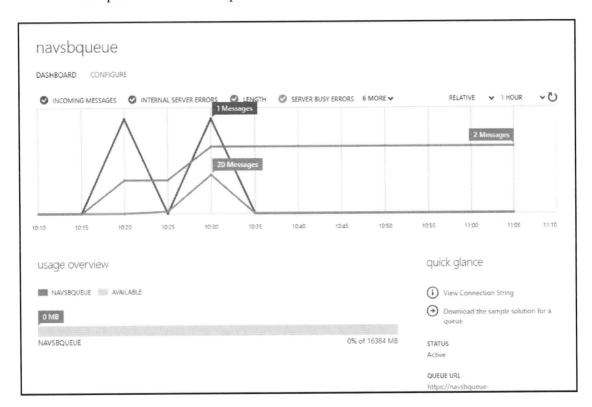

From a C# application, you can use a queue in this way (the code extract comes from my book, *Building ERP Solutions with Microsoft Dynamics NAV* by Packt Publishing):

A client application sends a message (`order` object) to the Azure Service Bus queue:

```
var client =
QueueClient.CreateFromConnectionString(ServiceBusConnectionString,
QueueName);
BrokeredMessage message = new BrokeredMessage(order, new
DataContractSerializer(typeof(ShopSalesOrder)));
client.Send(message);
```

The cloud service can retrieve the messages from the Azure Service Bus queue:

```
private static void ReceiveOrders()
        {
        Console.WriteLine("\nReceiving message from Azure Service
        Bus Queue...");
        try
        {
            var client =
            QueueClient.CreateFromConnectionString
            (ServiceBusConnectionString, QueueName);
            while (true)
            {
                try
                {
                    //receive messages from Queue
                    BrokeredMessage message =
                    client.Receive(TimeSpan.FromSeconds(5));
                    if (message != null)
                    {
                        //Retrieves the order object
                        Console.WriteLine(string.Format("Message
                        received: Id = {0} ", message.MessageId));
                        ShopSalesOrder orderReceived =
                        message.GetBody<ShopSalesOrder>(new
                        DataContractSerializer(typeof
                        (ShopSalesOrder)));
                         //Further custom message processing could
                         go here...
                        message.Complete();
                    }
                    else
                    {
                        //no more messages in the queue
                        break;
                    }
                }
                catch (MessagingException e)
                {
                    if (!e.IsTransient)
                    {
                        Console.WriteLine(e.Message);
                        throw;
                    }
                    else
                    {
                        HandleTransientErrors(e);
                    }
```

```
                    }
                }
            }
        catch(Exception ex)
        {
            //Handle exception here...
        }
    }
```

Compensating Transaction pattern

This pattern tries to solve a problem of a typical distributed system—transactional consistency.

A transaction could be defined as an action (or a series of coordinated actions) performed to fulfill a business functionality. This pattern tries to solve one of the problems of a typical distributed system—transactional consistency. In a distributed system (such as a cloud-based architecture), it's always very difficult to guarantee the consistency of a long-running transaction, so the idea of this pattern is to use a series of smaller individual transactions that can be undone (compensating transactions). In the Compensating Transaction pattern, the steps of a compensating transaction must undo the steps in the original operation.

In a cloud-based architecture, a transaction is not like a transaction on a database. When working with a database such as a SQL Server, if a transaction fails you can roll back the transaction to the original state. In a distributed cloud system, during a transaction of an instance of an application, other concurrent instances can change data, or if your transaction works on different cloud services, restoring the original state might not be so easy.

Imagine, for example, an application that calls a cloud service by passing data for validation, then updates an entity on a cloud database and after that, it sends a message to a queue. If one of these steps fail, the final business results could be affected.

As a definition, compensation is the process of restoring a system to its original state upon the occurrence of an error or a situation where the business transaction could not successfully proceed. The idea under the Compensating Transaction pattern is essentially this—when an operation starts, the application needs to record every step of the performed operation (if it was a success or not) and the steps to undo the work. When the transaction fails, the application can reverse the work by going back to each step and restoring the transaction to the original state.

This pattern should be used only when you have actions that must be undone (rolled back) if they fail.

An interesting C# implementation of this pattern can be found at this link: `https://github.com/flowing/flowing-trip-booking-saga-c-sharp`.

In my experience, using Azure Service Bus for handling the transaction compensation instead of implementing a workflow could be a valid approach. For each step of a transaction:

- The application sends a message to an Azure Service Bus with the transaction data and operation details
- The application performs the operation on the target service
- If the transaction step fails, the application can check the Azure Service Bus for restoring the entire transaction to the original state

Summary

In this chapter, we've analyzed the main architectural strategies and patterns in order to achieve Resiliency in a cloud architecture, and we've been given practical advice on how and when to implement them in your solutions.

In the next chapter, we'll see a new important aspect to take into consideration when implementing an Azure cloud architecture—identity and security management. We'll see best practices for security implementation in Azure, and the main cloud patterns for handling security in an Azure cloud environment.

9

Identity and Security

In the previous chapter, we analyzed the Azure Cloud patterns to achieve resiliency on your architecture's implementation.

The final chapter of the book will be focused on another important aspect to consider while implementing a cloud-based architecture—identity and security.

The following are the topics, which we will cover in this chapter:

- Security in the cloud
- Azure network security
- **Single sign-on** (**SSO**) and Multi-Factor Authentication (**MFA**)
- Azure MFA setup
- Federation and the Federated Identity pattern
- Gatekeeper pattern
- Valet Key pattern

Security in the cloud

When implementing a solution architecture (on-premise or in the cloud) the aspect of protecting your data and your identity from malicious attacks is always one of the first things to consider, and especially because of the cloud's nature to be considered as a *shared resource*, things like identity management, access control, and privacy management must have a very high priority on your design.

Cloud computing security can be defined as *a broad set of policies, technologies, and controls deployed to protect data, applications, and the associated infrastructure of cloud computing* (Wikipedia).

Implementing security in the cloud is quite similar to implementing security on-premises, the only difference being that in the cloud, you don't have the costs of maintaining the hardware infrastructure and you have the facilities that the cloud platform gives security features built-in without extra costs (the main cloud vendors such as Microsoft with Azure have a strong and always updated security platform).

When designing an application for the cloud, there are three main aspects to check:

- The application must restrict access to only authorized users
- The application must be designed and deployed securely and data protection must be guaranteed
- Sensitive data should always be protected

In order to improve the security of your Azure cloud infrastructure, there are some patterns and best practices that can be implemented when planning for a solution. In the upcoming sections, we'll see an overview of each of them.

Azure network security

Before talking about identity and authentication in the cloud, it's important to talk about Azure network security (the main topic of this chapter). I think it's necessary to say that when implementing a cloud infrastructure, the word *security* is not only related to managing identity and information, but also related to how your network in the cloud must be designed.

This is out of the scope of this book, but I think it's useful to remind you of some of the best practices that Microsoft recommends when you plan to design a network of resources on Azure:

- Logically segment subnets on your Azure virtual networks and use network security groups and Availability Sets.
- Control the routing behavior. By default, a virtual machine on an Azure virtual network can connect to other resources in the same network and have outbound communications with the internet. This is a default, but you can change this behavior if needed.
- Enable forced tunneling on your virtual machines when you have cross-premises connectivity between your Azure virtual network and your on-premises network.
- Use virtual network appliances if you need an extra level of security such as firewalls, intrusion detection/prevention, web filtering, and antivirus.

- Use DMZs for segmenting your network and improving security when needed.
- Avoid exposure to the internet with dedicated WAN links, but for cross-premises connections, it's recommended to use Azure ExpressRoute.
- Optimize uptime and performance by using load balancing.
- Use global load balancing (Azure Traffic Manager) when you have globally distributed applications. This guarantees that your application will be available, even when an entire data center might become unavailable (very remote probability but…).
- Disable direct RDP and SSH access to Azure Virtual Machines from the internet. For remote VM management, it's recommended to use point-to-site or site-to-site VPN or ExpressRoute (for WANs).
- Enable Azure Security Center for all your Azure deployments.

 For more information, this is the link for the always updated Microsoft's recommendation topics regarding Azure network security: `https://docs. microsoft.com/en-us/azure/security/azure-security-network- security-best-practices`.

SSO and MFA

Nowadays, if you use a home banking portal or other online services from providers such as Microsoft, Apple, or Google (just for an example), you already know that to authenticate for certain services you don't only need to insert your username and password, but an extra level of security is required. Your authentication in order to use the service has that extra step, and normally, it requires you to:

- Enter your credentials
- Provide a trusted device you own
- Receive a security code on the trusted device
- Re-enter this code on the login phase in order to be authenticated correctly

Azure provides these features via the Azure MFA service.

Azure MFA is a scalable and reliable solution (SLA 99.9%) that provides a two-step verification mechanism for authentication on Azure. It can be integrated with your on-premise Active Directory and with your custom applications and it's very easy to set up.

When Azure MFA is active and a user logs into an application, the second step of authentication is sent to the user. There are different verification methods with Azure MFA, which are explained as follows:

- **Phone call**: The user receives a call on the registered phone number, he must then enter a PIN and press #.
- **Text message**: The user receives a text message on the registered mobile phone with a 6-digit code that must then be inserted into the login page.
- **Mobile app notification**: A verification message is sent to the user's registered mobile phone. The user needs to enter a PIN and then click on a **Verify** button in the mobile app.
- **Mobile app verification code**: The mobile app on the user's phone displays a verification code (changes every 30 seconds). The user has to insert this code in the login page in order to be authenticated.
- **Third-party authentications**: You can configure Azure MFA to use other third-party verification methods.

These methods can be configured by users.

Azure MFA is offered at three different main levels:

- **Multifactor Authentication for Office 365**: This works only with Office 365 applications, managed from the Office 365 portal. This is totally free of charge.
- **Multifactor Authentication for Azure AD Administrators**: This is a feature that is free of charge for users who have the Global Administrator role in Azure AD tenants assigned.
- **Azure Multifactor Authentication (full)**: This includes the Azure Active Directory Premium and Enterprise Mobility plus Security plans. It's configurable via the Azure portal and can be activated in the cloud or on-premise.

 For a feature comparison between these MFA versions, I recommend checking this link: https://docs.microsoft.com/en-us/azure/multi-factor-authentication/multi-factor-authentication-versions-plans

From the Azure portal, you can set up MFA for a user in two different ways:

- **MFA always enabled for the user**: Every time the user performs a login request, they need to perform a two-step verification (the only exception is if the login is performed from a trusted IP).

- **MFA enabled with a conditional policy**: You can define a rule for the user (or for a group) and two-steps verification is required only if the rule condition is met. This method works only with Azure MFA in the cloud.

With Azure MFA active on Azure, a user can be in one of the following states:

- **Disabled**: The user is not active with Azure MFA. This is the default state.
- **Enabled**: The user has the Azure MFA feature activated, but it's not registered. At the next login, it will receive a prompt to register with MFA.
- **Enforced**: The user has the Azure MFA feature active and the registration process is completed.

Azure MFA setup

Configuring Azure MFA for your users is really very simple—just perform the following steps:

1. Sign in to the Azure portal with an administrator account and navigate to **Azure Active Directory** | **Users and Groups** | **All users**. Then, click on **Multi-factor Authentication**:

2. A new page will be opened where you can see the MFA status of each user. Here, you can bulk update the status for all your users or you can select the users for which you want to update their MFA status:

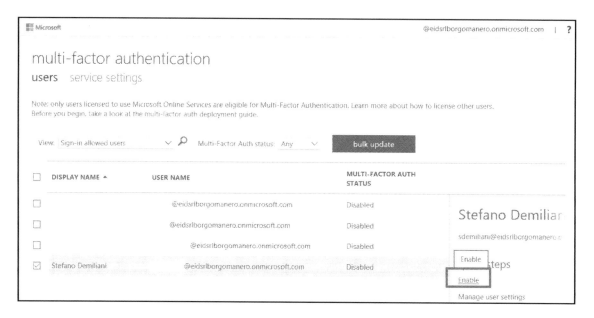

3. You can also manage this task with Azure Powershell (this is my recommended way if you need to activate MFA for a long list of users). With Azure Powershell, you can perform this task with a script like this:

```
    $users =
"user1@domain.com","user2@domain.com","user3@domain.com",
    "user4@domain.com"
    foreach ($user in $users)
    {
        $st = New-Object -TypeName
Microsoft.Online.Administration.StrongAuthenticationRequirement
        $st.RelyingParty = "*"
        $st.State = "Enabled"
        $sta = @($st)
        Set-MsolUser -UserPrincipalName $user
        -StrongAuthenticationRequirements $sta
    }
```

4. If you want to enable Azure MFA with a conditional policy, in the Azure portal, you need to select **Azure Active Directory** | **Conditional Access**:

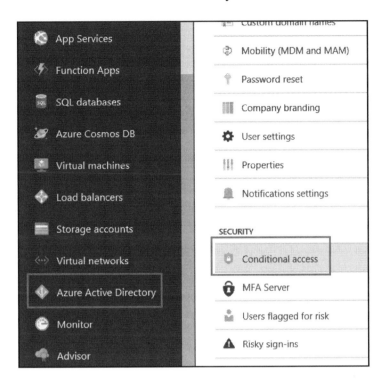

5. On the **Conditional access** blade, click on **Add** and then in the **New** blade, type the name of your new policy:

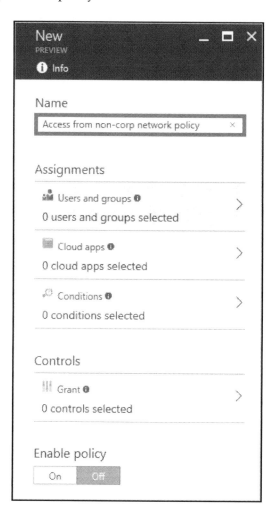

6. In the **Assignments** section, navigate to **Users and groups** | **Select users and groups** | **Select** and select your users:

7. Now, click on the **Cloud apps** section, then navigate to **Select apps** | **Select** and select your cloud app:

8. After that, select the **Conditions** section and then click on **Locations**. Here, click on **Yes** in the **Configure** section and **All locations** in the **Include** section:

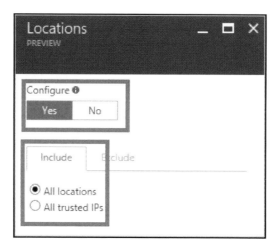

9. Then, click on the **Exclude** tab and check the **All Trusted IPs** checkbox (so your trusted IP addresses will be exempt from the policy implemented):

10. After confirming the operation (by clicking on the **Done** button), go back to the **Controls** option and click on **Grant**:

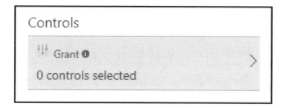

11. On the **Grant** option window, select the **Allow access** option and check **Require multi-factor authentication** and **Require all the selected controls**:

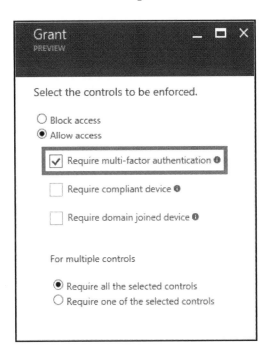

12. Now, as the last step, go back to the **New** blade, select **Enable policy** as **ON** and click on **Create** in order to create your conditional access policy:

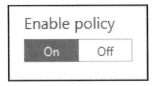

 For more details on conditional access activation, I recommend checking this link: https://docs.microsoft.com/en-us/azure/active-directory/active-directory-conditional-access-azure-portal

Federation and the Federated Identity Pattern

In many cloud scenarios, it's quite common that for the everyday business, your users need to work with different applications that comes from different providers and every application could have its own authentication mechanisms and credentials.

Imagine a business scenario where you have N different applications (on-premise applications, or cloud applications) and a user must have access to all of these N applications. In a standard environment, the user has to register in every application and remember every login accordingly.

As you can imagine, it could be quite difficult for an administrator to manage users and applications and users will have a better experience if they could use all these applications with the same credentials.

A solution for this scenario is to decouple authentication from authorization and (for authentication) using *federated identity*, where the user authentication must be delegated to a trusted identity provider.

The following picture shows a diagram of the **Federated Identity Pattern**:

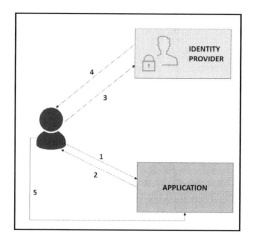

With this pattern, when a client **APPLICATION** needs to authenticate on a cloud service, the cloud service forwards the authentication request to an **IDENTITY PROVIDER**. The **IDENTITY PROVIDER** checks the client identity and returns a *Security Token* with information about the authenticated user (identity plus additional information such as roles). The client can then use this token to once again authenticate the final application.

The flow of the steps involved in authentication is as follows:

1. The user requests access to the **APPLICATION**
2. The **APPLICATION** redirects the user to an **IDENTITY PROVIDER**
3. The user authenticates itself with the **IDENTITY PROVIDER**
4. The **IDENTITY PROVIDER** returns a Security Token to the user
5. The user returns to the application with the Security Token and the application allows access to the user accordingly with the permission granted by the Security Token

The **IDENTITY PROVIDER** can also be included into an Identity Management application that integrates external identity providers such as Azure Active Directory, ADFS, and Social Identity Providers. This is a quite common real-world scenario nowadays.

This pattern has many advantages, which are as follows:

- It supports SSO different applications by eliminating the need for multiple login credentials for every application
- Roles management is more easy and centralized
- No internal overhead of identity management for the cloud service (this task is provided by the **IDENTITY PROVIDER**)
- Authentication is decoupled from authorization—the Identity Provider is responsible for authentication, the application itself is responsible for the authorization
- More sophisticated authentication mechanisms (such as Two-Factor authentication, Multi-Factor authentication and so on) can be implemented in a central way (no need to implement them at the application level)
- You can grant access to your applications also to users that are external to your corporate

There's one big issue with this pattern—the **IDENTITY PROVIDER** could be a single point of failure. If it's not available, your applications will not work because no authentication will be provided. It's extremely important that the **IDENTITY PROVIDER** is an *always up* service, so it's better that this is managed by someone (like Microsoft) that can guarantee a high level of SLA.

With the Azure platform, you can implement federation on your cloud architecture using **Active Directory Federation Services** (**AD FS**). This provides a platform for having simplified, secured identity federation and single sign-on capabilities with cloud applications. A federation with Azure AD or Office 365 permits you to enable your users to use on-premise credentials in order to access all resources in the cloud.

Deploying AD FS in Azure permits you to have a centralized management of your network (via the Azure portal), permits you have scalability and high availability (by using Availability Sets), and also redundancy.

 For information about deploying Active Directory Federation Services in Azure, I recommend you to start from this link: https://docs.microsoft.com/en-us/azure/active-directory/connect/active-directory-aadconnect-azure-adfs

Gatekeeper pattern

When a client application sends a request to a service, it's quite common that this service handles authentication, the processing of the incoming request, and the access to other services (resources) required to satisfy the incoming request.

In a cloud environment, in order to improve the overall security of the system, it could be useful to split this behavior into two different layers:

- A layer that handles the incoming request
- A layer that processes the request and provides access to other resources

This architectural pattern is called **Gatekeeper pattern**. With this pattern, between the **CLIENT** and the **CLOUD SERVICES** that handle the requests, there's an extra layer (the **GATEKEEPER**) that validates and sanitizes the incoming requests.

The Gatekeeper pattern can be represented as follows:

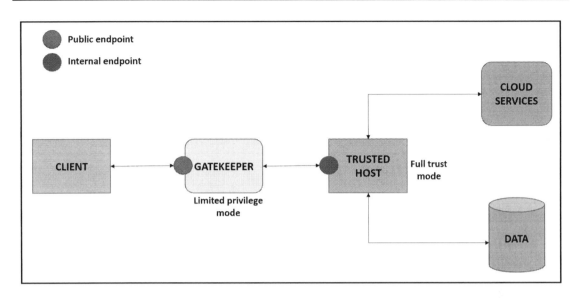

When this pattern is implemented, a client sends an incoming request for a cloud service to the *Gatekeeper* public endpoint. The Gatekeeper service is limited to handle only the validation of the incoming request (no processing) and it rejects requests that do not meet the validation requirements. The Gatekeeper has no access to credentials and keys. It's typically recommended that this service runs in a limited privilege mode (no access to other cloud resources or to the trusted host).

When the Gatekeeper validates the incoming request, it forwards the request to the trusted host (the destination cloud service) that handles the processing of the request (it can call an internal endpoint of the trusted host or it could place a message on a queue for an extra level of decoupling). Only the trusted host can have access to other cloud services (such as storage services).

The benefits of using this pattern is that you can decouple the validation of the incoming requests to the processing of them. Your cloud architecture will expose to the external clients only the public endpoint of the Gatekeeper, while all the other cloud services are not visible to the outside world.

As you can imagine, the Gatekeeper could be a single point of failure on your architecture. If this service is down, requests are not validated and their processing will not be performed. In order to avoid this (and to improve the overall scalability of the solution), it's recommended to have more than one instance of the gatekeeper service (or use autoscaling).

For implementing this pattern on Azure, you can use services such as **Azure Application Gateway** (https://docs.microsoft.com/en-us/azure/application-gateway/) and **Azure API Management** (https://azure.microsoft.com/en-us/services/api-management/).

An Azure Application Gateway provides a full set of features for application delivery control and can be created via the Azure portal by navigating to **Networking | Application Gateway**:

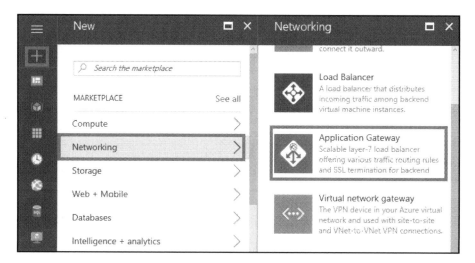

Azure API Management services permits you to publish custom APIs to the cloud. An API is based on a set of operations available for developers and each API can be added to one or more products (the final package on which APIs are surfaced to developers). To use an API, developers subscribe to a product that contains that API, and then they can call the API's operation. Each API contains also a reference to the backend service that implements the API, and its operations map to the operations implemented by the backend service itself.

Azure API Management service is composed of the following components:

- **API gateway**: This is the endpoint that accepts the calls to the APIs, validates them, and routes them to your backend.
- **Publisher portal**: This is the interface where you can setup your API, policies for access and users.
- **Developer portal**: This is a portal for developers that use the APIs. Here, they can read the API's documentation, make API subscriptions for using them, and test an API.

To create a new Azure API Management service instance, on the Azure portal perform the following steps:

1. Navigate to **New** | **Enterprise Integration** | **API management**:

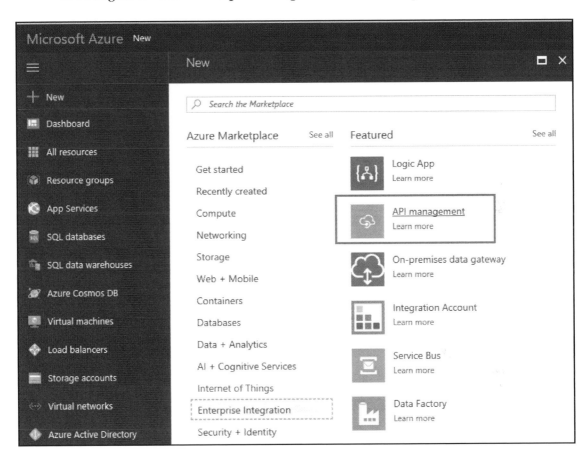

2. In the **API Management Service** blade, select a name for your API (that must be unique) and complete the settings.

The **Organization name** is used in the title in the developer portal for the API and also as the sender name for notification emails. These emails will be sent to the **Administrator email** address you have specified in this window. Here, as a **Pricing tier (View full pricing details)** I've selected **Developer (No SLA)**. This is only for evaluation and test; this must not be used in production.

3. Click on **Create** to create your **API Management service**.

4. Now that the service is in place, you can select your **API Management service** instance and import your custom API. (It's better if you've deployed it before as an Azure website.) When your API is imported, you can see and test all the methods:

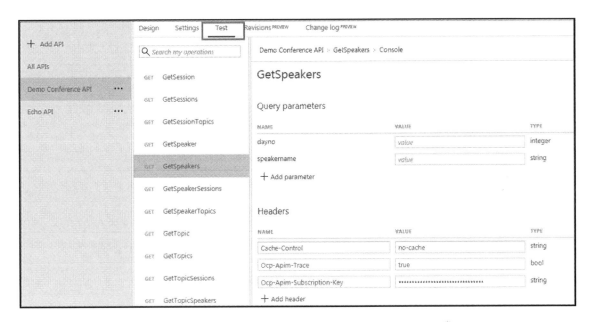

5. You also have access to the **Publisher portal** and **Developer portal** previously described:

6. When an operation is invoked from the **Developer portal**, you can see its response status, response headers, and response content.

Valet Key pattern

Another way of adding an extra layer of security to your cloud-based solution is using security tokens to access specific cloud resources.

As an example, let's consider a client application that sends a request to a cloud application. In this request, the cloud application needs to retrieve a Blob file from a cloud data store and returns them to the client:

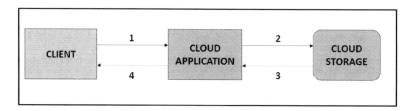

We can handle this scenario with the Gatekeeper pattern, but in particular types of scenario, in order to increase the overall performances of the architecture, we could directly permit the data store to handle the streaming of data, bypassing the extra processing of the cloud service:

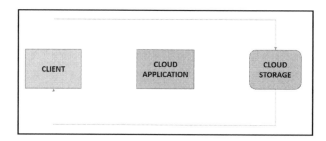

The Valet Key pattern diagram can be represented as shown in the following figure:

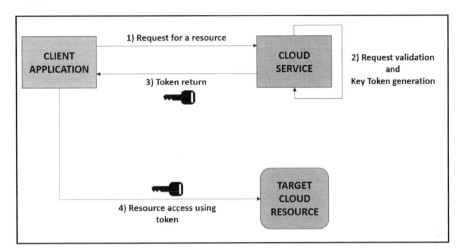

With the Valet Key pattern, the client application request for a resource to a cloud service. The cloud service checks for the validity of the request, generates a key token (*valet key*) and returns this token to the client application.

This token has the main feature: providing a time-limited and feature-limited access to a specific cloud resource. The client application can now access the target cloud resource by using the valet key token. On the target resource, the client application can perform only the operations that are permitted by the security token (for example, only download a certain Blob from a data store).

The client can access the cloud target resource only for a specific period of time. After that period, the valet key token becomes invalid and the access to the target resource will be denied.

As you can see, by implementing this pattern, you can guarantee a simplified managing access to cloud resources (no need to direct user configuration and authentication) and time-limit permission.

You can use this pattern in Azure when implementing solution architectures that use Azure Storage by using Shared Access Signatures. With this feature, you can grant access to an Azure Storage entity without the need to explicitly create a grant for the client application or share your account key. The client application receives a shared key with grants (permissions and time limit). It can perform the authorized operation on the storage entity and then the permissions will be released.

The Shared Access Signature is a special signed URI composed by a storage resource URI and by a SAS token (generated at the client side) that contains a signature and resources that the client application can access:

https://storagesample.blob.core.windows.net/sample-container/sampleBlob.txt?sv=2015-07-08&sr=b&sig=39Up9JzHkxhUthFEjEH9594DJxe7w6cIRCgOV6ICGSo%3D&se=2016-10-18T21%3A51%3A37Z&sp=rcw

Storage Resource URI   SAS Token

For more information on how to create a SAS token, check this link: `https://docs.microsoft.com/en-us/azure/storage/common/storage-dotnet-shared-access-signature-part-1#sas-examples`

There are two types of shared access signatures in Azure:

- **Service Shared Access Signature**: This permits access to a resource in only one storage service (Queue, Table, Blob, or File service).

For more information see *Constructing a Service SAS* at this link: `https://msdn.microsoft.com/library/dn140255.aspx`

- **Account Shared Access Signature**: This permits access to a resource in one or more storage services and you can delegate access to operations.

For more information see *Constructing an Account SAS* at this link: `https://msdn.microsoft.com/library/mt584140.aspx`

Now we can see an example on how to generate a shared access signature for a Blob storage and generate a previously described access policy for implementing the pattern in a real scenario.

On my Azure subscription, I've created a Blob storage account with a container:

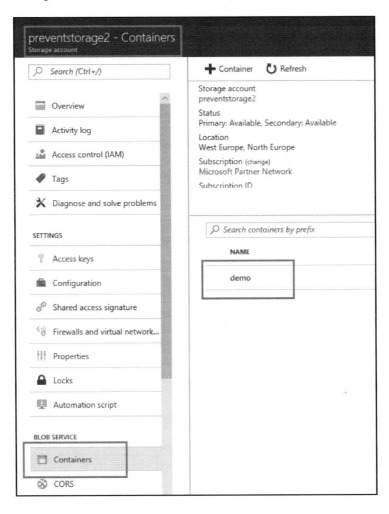

Let's open Visual Studio and create a new C# console application. After that, we need to add a reference to the *Azure Storage Client library* package (right-click on *Reference* and select **Manage NuGet packages**):

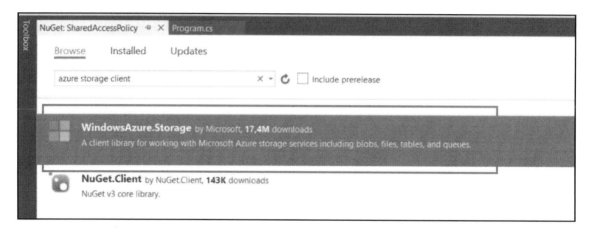

Also, provide a reference to the **Microsoft.WindowsAzure.ConfigurationManager** package:

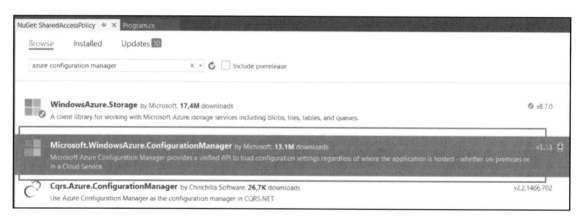

In this application, we perform the following steps:

1. Connect to the storage account
2. Retrieve a reference to the container
3. Generate a Shared Access Signature for the container, with only an expiry time and list and write permissions

The code for the application is as follows:

```
class Program
    {
        static void Main(string[] args)
        {
            //Read the Storage Account connection string from
            App.config
            CloudStorageAccount storageAccount =
            CloudStorageAccount.Parse(CloudConfigurationManager.
            GetSetting("AzureStorageConnectionString"));
            //Create the blob service client
            CloudBlobClient blobClient =
            storageAccount.CreateCloudBlobClient();
            //Reference to storage account container
            CloudBlobContainer blobContainer =
blobClient.GetContainerReference("demo");
            blobContainer.CreateIfNotExists();
            //Generate a Shared Access Signature URI for the storage
account Blob container
            Console.WriteLine("Generated Container SAS URI: " +
                            GenerateBlobContainerSASUri(blobContainer));
            Console.ReadLine();
        }

        //Shared Access Signature generation
        static string GenerateBlobContainerSASUri(CloudBlobContainer
blobContainer)
        {
            //SAS policy with constraints and time-limit setup
            SharedAccessBlobPolicy sasPolicy = new
SharedAccessBlobPolicy();
            sasPolicy.SharedAccessExpiryTime =
DateTimeOffset.UtcNow.AddHours(12);
            sasPolicy.Permissions = SharedAccessBlobPermissions.List |
                                    SharedAccessBlobPermissions.Write;
            //SAS token creation
            string sasToken =
blobContainer.GetSharedAccessSignature(sasPolicy);
            //Final SAS URI
            return blobContainer.Uri + sasToken;
        }
    }
```

The Shared Access Signature for the container is created by the
`GenerateBlobContainerSASUri` function and it's available immediately (no start time
setup).

When you run the application, this is the final result:

You obtain a SAS URI that the client application can use to access the cloud resource (storage account container).

As described earlier, we can generate a Shared Access Signature also for a single Blob in a storage account container.

To do so, we can create a method similar to the following:

```
static string GenerateBlobSASUri(CloudBlobContainer blobContainer)
        {
            //Sets a reference to a blob inside the container in input
            CloudBlockBlob blob =
            blobContainer.GetBlockBlobReference("demo.txt");
            //Creates a blob file (or updates it if existing)
            string blobContent = "Demo Blob file created for Packt
            Publishing.";
            blob.UploadText(blobContent);
            //SAS policy setup for the blob file (permissions and time-
            limits)
            SharedAccessBlobPolicy sasPolicy = new
            SharedAccessBlobPolicy();
            sasPolicy.SharedAccessStartTime =
            DateTimeOffset.UtcNow.AddMinutes(-3);
            sasPolicy.SharedAccessExpiryTime =
            DateTimeOffset.UtcNow.AddHours(12);
            sasPolicy.Permissions = SharedAccessBlobPermissions.Read |
            SharedAccessBlobPermissions.Write;
            //SAS Token generation
            string sasToken = blob.GetSharedAccessSignature(sasPolicy);
            //Final SAS URI
            return blob.Uri + sasToken;
        }
```

In the `Main` function of our Console application, we can call the function to generate the SAS key:

```
//Shared Access Signature generation for a specific blob inside a Blob
Storage container
Console.WriteLine("Blob specific SAS URI: " +
GenerateBlobSASUri(blobContainer));
```

As described in the pattern, an application that wants to use the storage has to first request the shared access key. When a shared access key is obtained, the application can perform operations on the storage container.

As an example, this is a function that a client application can use to perform operations on a Blob file in the previous container after having the Shared Access Key:

```
//Function for testing the usage of a SAS key for a blob
static void TestBlobSAS(string SASuri)
        {
        //Gets a blob reference from the SAS uri
        CloudBlockBlob blob = new CloudBlockBlob(new Uri(SASuri));
        //WRITE operation test
        try
        {
            string blobContent = "Write test with SAS token for
            Packt.";
            MemoryStream msWrite = new
            MemoryStream(Encoding.UTF8.GetBytes(blobContent));
            msWrite.Position = 0;
            using (msWrite)
            {
                blob.UploadFromStream(msWrite);
            }
            Console.WriteLine("Write operation completed
            successfully");
        }
        catch (StorageException e)
        {
            Console.WriteLine("Write operation failed: " +
            e.Message);
        }
        //READ operation test
        try
        {
            MemoryStream msRead = new MemoryStream();
            using (msRead)
            {
                blob.DownloadToStream(msRead);
```

```
                    msRead.Position = 0;
                    using (StreamReader reader = new
                    StreamReader(msRead, true))
                    {
                        string line;
                        while ((line = reader.ReadLine()) != null)
                        {
                            Console.WriteLine(line);
                        }
                    }
                }
                Console.WriteLine("Read operation completed
                successfully.");
            }
            catch (StorageException e)
            {
                Console.WriteLine("Read operation failed: " +
                e.Message);
            }
            //DELETE operation test
            try
            {
                blob.Delete();
                Console.WriteLine("Delete operation completed
                successfully");
            }
            catch (StorageException e)
            {
                Console.WriteLine("Delete operation failed: " +
                e.Message);
            }
        }
```

In this function, we perform different operations (`write`, `read`, and `delete`) on the blob file using the SAS URI previously retrieved.

If the URI (provided by the client application) grants the operation on the blob in the container, the task is performed successfully; otherwise, the client application receives an exception (`StorageException`).

Summary

In this chapter, we have analyzed the main cloud patterns in order to guarantee identity and security when implementing cloud-based architectures with Azure. We have seen the benefits of each of them (with examples) and I hope that, after reading this book, you now have the knowledge of what you have to check and to do when you're implementing a real-world solution with the Azure platform.

We're at the end of this book. I hope that your mind is now more open in order to be a successful cloud architect.

Other Books You May Enjoy

If you enjoyed this book, you may be interested in these other books by Packt:

Azure for Architects

Ritesh Modi

ISBN: 978-1-78839-739-1

- Familiarize yourself with the components of the Azure Cloud platform
- Understand the cloud design patterns
- Use enterprise security guidelines for your Azure deployment
- Design and implement Serverless solutions
- See Cloud architecture and the deployment pipeline
- Understand cost management for Azure solutions

Implementing Azure Solutions

Florian Klaffenbach, Jan-Henrik Damaschke, Oliver Michalski

ISBN: 978-1-78646-785-0

- Implement virtual networks, network gateways, Site-to-Site VPN, ExpressRoute, routing, and network devices
- Understand the working of different storage accounts in Azure
- Plan, deploy, and secure virtual machines
- Deploy and manage Azure Containers
- Get familiar with some common Azure usage scenarios

Leave a review - let other readers know what you think

Please share your thoughts on this book with others by leaving a review on the site that you bought it from. If you purchased the book from Amazon, please leave us an honest review on this book's Amazon page. This is vital so that other potential readers can see and use your unbiased opinion to make purchasing decisions, we can understand what our customers think about our products, and our authors can see your feedback on the title that they have worked with Packt to create. It will only take a few minutes of your time, but is valuable to other potential customers, our authors, and Packt. Thank you!

Index

37065248R00166

Printed in Great Britain
by Amazon